CALLED AND CHOSEN FOR DESTINY

KNOWING & FULFILLING YOUR DESTINY IN GOD

JOAN E. MURRAY

Joan Murray Ministries & Seeds Of Hope Worldwide Missions
26340 FM 1736
Waller, TX 77848
281-398-2501

PRAISE FOR CALLED AND CHOSEN
FOR DESTINY
KNOWING & FULFILLING YOUR DESTINY
IN GOD

~

JOAN GIVES you incredible insight to understanding God's calling and destiny for your life. I have no doubt *Called and Chosen for Destiny* will act as a compass to help you navigate through life on the journey to your destination.

Rudy Beltran, Pastor,

Destiny Through Christ Church, McAllen, TX

~

I have had the privilege of working closely with Joan at Lakewood Church and co-teaching a large Bible study class with her. She is a gifted, seasoned minister and a powerfully anointed teacher of the Word of God. She is qualified to minister at any level anywhere in the world. I know God is going to use Joan to impact countless lives around the world.

Steve Austin, Member Care Pastor,

Lakewood Church, Houston, TX

∾

A Bible scholar, prayer warrior, and disciple of Jesus Christ, Joan exemplifies the Word as it is written in 1 Corinthians 7:32–34. I am inspired by her discipline, diligence, and consistency in work, rest, and devotional time with the Lord.

Dr. Ellecya McCants
Sitrem Turner Group, Wellness Consultants

∾

The search for purpose and significance has been a dilemma that has plagued humanity since the beginning of time. 'Who am I and why was I created?' are questions that each of us must answer if we are to fulfill our God given destiny. In her book, *Called and Chosen for Destiny: Knowing and Fulfilling Your Destiny in God,* Ms. Murray gives practical insights on determining your God ordained destiny. All who read her book will instantly realize that they have many God inspired insights that will make their lives richer.

Raymond H. Hillis, M. Div., Pastor
Progressive Missionary Baptist Church

ACKNOWLEDGMENTS

~

My heartfelt thanks to the Holy Spirit, my friend and teacher, who inspired the writing of this book, and who constantly reminded me that I was the note taker, while He was the writer, so I could trust His leading.

I thank my family for allowing me to grow and develop in my relationship with the Lord and for never questioning my claims concerning His directions for my life.

To the Board of Directors of Joan Murray Ministries: Rebecca James, Ellecya McCants, Roy & Joan Sugawa, and Cynthia Thompson, sincere thanks for your words of encouragement and your amazing support.

My sincere thanks to the Joan Murray Ministries team who work tirelessly to make these ministries a success. I appreciate all you do to help me change lives around the world.

Thanks to my editors, Cynthia Thompson, Julia Rigos, Joan Sugawa, and the editorial staff at Tate Publishing for doing such outstanding work. I will be forever grateful to the Young Women Auxiliary at Progressive Missionary Baptist Church in Houston, Texas, who was so receptive to the teachings of the Called and Chosen series.

I am extremely thankful to Lakewood Church New Direction Compass class for always being there and for their readiness to receive the messages/teachings that the Lord gives me.

My sincere appreciation to Tina Underwood, of Captive No More, for her wisdom and insight from the Lord concerning the teaching series and the book.

Finally, my heartfelt thanks to my friends and supporters for their prayers and support of the ministries.

CONTENTS

FOREWORD

~

ONE OF THE GREATEST pursuits of the human heart is for a sense of purpose and spiritual fulfillment. This pursuit can take many forms and is manifested in hundreds of ways, but until it is satisfied, there will always be a sense of emptiness in the recesses of the soul. It is this pursuit that has given birth to religion, which has produced a buffet of spiritual alternatives for the hungry human heart. However, over the past thirty years, I have traveled to over fifty nations, speaking on the subject of spirituality, personal purpose, and fulfillment, and have come to the conclusion that religion and its smorgasbord of customs, traditions, and rituals preoccupies the seeker but does not fully answer the deep cry of the human spirit.

It is my conviction that the only solution to this human dilemma is the discovery of your personal purpose and sense of destiny. This is only possible through the cultivation of a personal relationship with the Creator of all things. This discovery is not a matter of religion but rather of reconciliation. The spiritual vacuum, which plagues every human spirit, is a result of the detachment of mankind from his Creator through the disobedience of his forefather, Adam. Ever since that tragic moment, the desire and craving of the human spirit has been for a relationship with his source, the Creator. The desire to discover a destiny for life is the ultimate motivation of mankind.

Joan Murray, in this work, *Called and Chosen for Destiny: Knowing and Fulfilling Your Destiny in God,* presents one of the most profound, yet simple dissertations on the priority, necessity, demand, and requirement for a dynamic, practical, effective, and daily relationship with our Creator God to lead to the discovery of a personal destiny. Her positive and human-friendly approach to this highly spiritual subject draws the reader into a world of possibilities and increases the appetite for the presence and power of God in your life, manifesting a strong sense of destiny in your life.

Her presentation of the different aspects of the concept of destiny and the process for fulfilling that destiny is refreshing and inspires you to want to learn more and pursue your future. The principles and precepts contained in these pages are biblically sound and humanly possible. Joan leaps over complicated theological hurdles and theoretical distractions and delivers the day-by-day practice of cultivating a real, practical roadmap for personal success. It is my belief that this book will become a classic and will assist all who desire to fill the void in their hearts and spirits for a personal and true sense of destiny.

I challenge you to proceed to the following pages and peel away the wisdom embedded in each sentence and let the power of destiny that is available to all who believe explode in your life daily.

—Dr. Myles E. Munroe
Nassau, Bahamas

INTRODUCTION

~

AS I THINK BACK over my life, I have wondered many times why my existence seemed so ordinary. I have had a clear understanding that God handcrafted me for a great destiny but have often felt that my existence was merely mediocre. Like me, I know that many of you have a great desire to step out of the ordinary and into something extraordinary, fulfilling, and beneficial. You desire to step into greatness but are unsure of the steps that will lead you down the path to ultimate fulfillment. As I contemplated my ordinary existence, I came to realize that ordinary was not for me, and it should not be for you either. It was liberating to discover that if I were the only person on earth, God would still have sent Jesus, and He would have died that painful and horrible death just for me. The same holds true for you as well.

I came to understand that a loving Father had adopted me into His family. This adoption came because His Son was willing to be born into an earthly family where He became the adopted Son of a carpenter. By His death, He provided a way for us to be adopted by God. It was also great news when I discovered that in previous centuries, although a natural-born son could be disinherited, a son or daughter by adoption could never be disinherited. God Himself has adopted and given you His name, an inheritance, and a destiny, and He will never abandon nor disinherit you. He has provided you an opportunity to walk away from a mediocre and ordinary existence into a great calling and an even greater destiny. God has called, chosen, and destined you to live a life brimming with an abundance of joy, peace, health, and wealth. As you discover this life, which is filled with destiny, you will discover something beyond the ordinary.

Many times, on the way to your destiny, you may encounter some disappointments, discouragement, and even despair, which have been sent by the enemy to derail and keep you living below your privileges as heirs to a great inheritance. However, as sons and daughters of God, you must know who you are and understand your rightful place. You are children of the King and are designed for greatness in Him. Therefore, you must be tenacious and determined in your heart that you will not be stopped, deterred, or derailed. You will be victorious in all areas of life and will fulfill the great calling and destiny that God has placed on your life.

The book you hold in your hand contains signposts to help you achieve your greatest destiny in God. It is my passion to help people realize how truly valuable they are, and the high price God paid to get them back into a right relationship with Him. If you truly desire to experience fullness in your life and to walk completely in God's amazing blessings and provisions for your destiny, you must fully accept how greatly loved you are.

As you read, believe, and apply the principles and insights from this book, expect God to take you into a deeper, more intimate relationship with Him. In this new intimacy, you will discover a new and deeper level of your purpose, your passion, and your life's calling. You will discover that God desires your total fulfillment in every area of your life. I, therefore, invite you to dig deeply into the pages of this book to discover the roadmap that will lead you on an adventure to your destination, which will be worth your pursuit and your total commitment.

Joan E. Murray

OTHER BOOKS BY:

JOAN E. MURRAY

Boldness in Christ

Broken, Yet Unstoppable

Called and Chosen for Destiny

Discovering God Vol. 1

Discovering God Vol. 2

Faith That Conquers

Flow Through Me, Lord

Freedom In The Son

Hope In Difficult Seasons

I MUST PRAY

Lord, Make Me Whole

Overcoming Loneliness and Aloneness

Reconnect

Señor, Hazme Íntegro

Show Me How to Love

Time in Life's Waiting Room

Winning In The Battles of Life

Worship, Our Deepest Need

You Can TRUST Him

GOD HAS CALLED AND CHOSEN YOU FOR GREAT DESTINY IN HIM

~

"When God calls you, you must be willing to obey and step out in faith even though you may not understand where the road will lead."

Joan E. Murray, Author

1. CALLED BY GOD

FROM AN EARLY AGE, I sensed that there was so much more to life than what I had yet experienced. I felt there were greater things to accomplish but I was unsure of what they were. I have consistently felt that mediocrity was not for me and that I was in no way designed for an ordinary existence. I have been persistent in my conversations with God that there must be more to life than this. If you have ever felt that you are living an average existence, living from day to day with no end in sight, and would like to yell at the top of your lungs, "Deliver me from this mediocrity!" Then this book is definitely for you! In this book, you will explore the truth that God has not called you to insignificance, but He has called and chosen you for greatness. Let us go on a journey to discover the process of fulfilling this great calling.

As I began my search, I wondered if God had something for me to do, and if so, what was delaying my getting to it. It seemed as if I had been in a holding pattern, waiting and waiting with seemingly no end in sight. I finally concluded that I did not have a full understanding of this great God that I serve and of His perfect timing for my life. I began the journey of a lifetime to discover what God had planned for me. This book journals what I discovered along the way.

My journey began when I first realized that God had called me out of darkness and into a place filled with His light. In this place of darkness where I had lived, I was filled with doubt, fear, and unbelief concerning whether there was a purpose for my existence. And if there was, could God really use me for something great in His Kingdom? When I began my search, I had been a Christian for several years but was dissatisfied and unhappy with where I was in my Christian walk. I went to church, prayed often, and served faithfully, and yet was experiencing a severe lack of fulfillment. There was such a feeling of drought in my life that I yearned for something more. I truly understood how great a salvation God had provided for me through the shed blood of Jesus and felt guilty that I was not content with His provision. I was later to discover that this drought, this deep yearning, was a desire for a deeper and more intimate relationship with God.

As I began reaching for more in this relationship, I still experienced times of frustration and disappointment because I was comparing myself with others' apparent satisfaction in Him while I was still exhibiting signs of discontentment. I wept much and questioned others frequently about their contentment and the source of it. I learned that many felt that they were living out the purposes for which God had called them, but they could not necessarily explain how they had arrived at these purposes or the process of getting there. It was through that search that I realized the answers could be found in no one but God. I went to Him with my concerns, and over a period of time, He began to unveil Himself and His plans to me.

My discovery of His plans began one night at church. I arrived early before the service started and began to observe people as they entered the sanctuary. I looked for signs of contentment on their faces and pondered the level of their fulfillment. Some people seemed exhausted and simply dragged themselves into the sanctuary because it was the mid-week service. It seemed that others came because they were not given an option. Yet there were some who had a bounce in their step. They seemed excited to be in the sanctuary and happy to be called into the presence of God. I decided that I wanted to be in this latter group, so my search began. This search started with my asking God to fill me with more of Himself. I increased my personal prayer time, and He began to make deposits of His promises and provisions into my heart. I learned through the Word that God had a plan and a call for every life, and I was determined to find His plan and calling for me. In my study of the Word, I discovered many answers within its pages as well as during times spent in prayer. The Lord began to surround me with like-minded people, who also had a desire for more of Him, and to discover His plans for their lives. This led me into many discussions and some great discoveries that I will share throughout this book.

One of those discoveries came in a conversation I had with a friend. She shared that her husband thought she was ungrateful and discontent with what God had given them. What her husband failed to realize was that she was indeed grateful for what God had done so far in her life, but there was this *knowing* that there was much more that she was called to than what she was currently experiencing. This sense of dissatisfaction was the tugging of God on her heart not to settle but to seek after Him for more of the blessings, provisions, and the destiny He had mapped out for her life. A longing to do and attain more was placed there by a loving Father who would not allow her to settle for an unremarkable existence. Discovering this opened my eyes anew to the realization that many people may be discontent in their Christian walk because they do not fully understand that God has a great plan and calling for their lives. His great plan and calling require that you get into His presence to find out how to truly live and enjoy life to its fullest. As you explore the reasons God has called you, ask the Holy Spirit to make His plans crystal clear to your heart.

To Be Called... *that you may declare the praises of Him who called you out of darkness into His wonderful light.*

1 Peter 2:9b (NIV)

All of you have been called by God to accomplish great things with your lives. He has called you to be a part of something greater than what you could ever imagine or think. You have been programmed by God with the desire to reach for more than just the things you have already attained. It seems, however, that this "something" keeps eluding you. I have discovered in my journey that the desire you have for more is the desire to know God at a deeper level and in a more intimate way. As you get to know Him, you will begin to discover the greater things that you feel a longing to attain. Before you were born, He called and made an appointment with you for the fulfillment of your destiny (Jeremiah 1:5).

You have been called, sanctified, and set apart for use by God. He called and selected you above all others to do something for Him. You are His preferred and chosen child whom He singled out for a specific assignment that only you can fulfill. In singling you out, He wants you to understand that you are made of the finest quality materials.

You are made in the likeness of the Father, Son, and Holy Spirit. Since you are created in Their Image, you have the backing and support you need to ultimately fulfill the calling on your life.

To be called means that the voice of God reached out from

heaven and arrested you along the journey of life. His invitation was so clear that you responded with a heartfelt decision to accept and accomplish great things for His Kingdom. His call to you answered a longing in your heart not only to do more but also to be more. His call summoned you to a closer view of His plans for your life, and as you caught a glimpse of what He proposed, your heart responded with a resounding "Yes!" Your "yes" signified that you were waiting to embrace His call and were ready to be trained and prepared for His ultimate use. He called, and you answered. In answering, you yielded your will to His will, your ways to His way, and your plans to His plan. As a result, you are now set apart and sanctified for His use. Repeat this out loud to yourself: "I am called, sanctified, and set apart for God's use. I am the preferred choice. I am singled out, and I am of the finest quality." Say this to yourself until you believe it and it takes root in the soil of your heart. Accept and embrace the calling of God for your life.

Many are Called

For many are called ... Matthew 22:14a (KJV)

The Bible specifically states that many are called. Before God called and selected you, you were lost, alone, and far away from Him. Then His voice resounded throughout the earth calling you into a relationship with Him. In this relationship, you have complete access into His Presence and can share your heart, your desires, and your concerns with Him. As you open yourself to Him, He will share the reason for His call and the great plans He has for your life. Understand that God calls out to all humanity. He does not limit His call to just a few. Everyone that God created received this call to share the riches of His Kingdom. He called you for a specific destiny that He has programmed you to fulfill. His call is an invitation for you to come and hear more about your destiny.

Consider Adam and Eve, the first people who received this call from God. When they heard His call, they must have responded quickly and with great excitement. I imagine that they had great expectations about having an audience with the Creator. They would have an opportunity to meet with Him face-to-face so that He could speak His destiny for them directly into their hearts. In their meetings with Him, they would have learned how to rule and govern the planet. Since God is all-knowing, He knew that they would not fully embrace the call that He had placed on their lives. He also knew that though they responded to His call initially, they would subsequently answer another call, which would ultimately lead them away from His plans and provisions for them and mankind.

Throughout Bible history and before the birth of Jesus, God has called and used great men and women to accomplish amazing things in His Kingdom. He called them by placing dreams, visions, and desires in their hearts. As they began to live out their dreams, they found that this was the purpose for which they had been born. Before reading any further, consider what dream He has called you to fulfill. While considering the dream, take it a step further by asking yourself this question: "If I knew that I ultimately could not fail, what would I be doing right now?" Just like you, I have considered this question. I discovered that I would be sharing the love of God with you and writing about His great plans for your life. How about you? What would your dreams be? I assure you that as you start to dream; and put movement to them by stepping out in faith and embracing the direction of God for your life; while attempting to fulfill these dreams; you will have the backing of the Godhead, and the heavenly host cheering you all the way to the finish line. Try it and listen for the cheers that go up as you begin.

The Planting of the Dreams

Are you wondering where your dreams and calling come from? How Abraham, Joseph, Rahab, and modern-day men and women have fulfilled such great destinies? God planted dreams into the soil of their hearts before they were born. Those dreams are God's vision for His children. I call them "hidden treasures" that you and I must dig for. They are hidden treasures because they are not just lying on the surface waiting for you to find them. Many of you have spent a lifetime doing many different things that have brought no fulfillment, and all the while you were in search of the "thing" that would complete your life. As you begin to think and meditate on what it is that you are called to do, let me give you some clues for the search.

As a child, what were some of the things that you loved doing? How about those things which came naturally to you, and were so easy for you to do that they were almost automatic? What things were you passionate about and are still passionate about today? If you can recall what those things are, then this will be a good place to begin this treasure hunt that will lead you into fulfilling your calling and destiny.

> *"It's all right," he said. "Don't be afraid. Your God, the God of your father, has given you treasure in your sacks." Genesis 43:23a (NIV)*

> *The Lord shall open unto thee His good treasure, the heaven to give the rain unto thy land in His season, and to bless all the work of thine hand: and thou shalt lend unto many nations, and thou shalt not borrow.*
> *Deuteronomy 28:12 (KJV)*

It is clear from these scriptures that God has a plan to bless your life with His rare and beautiful treasures. In fact, He has called you to enjoy His treasures here on earth. The scriptures above encourage you not to be afraid, not to hold back, and not to worry because He is your God, and He will fill your sacks. In modern-day vernacular—He will fill your checking account, your savings account, your home, and your life with rare and marvelous treasures. He further states that He is not going to provide from just any source, but He is going to open heaven, His storehouse of treasures, and rain down wisdom, insight, ideas, concepts, revelations, and prosperity into your heart and mind. God is saying that all the works of your hands will be prosperous. The reason simply is that when God called you, He did so to bless your life. When you are willing to use whatever provisions He gives you in service to Him, it is impossible for you not to experience His blessings.

My Call and Treasure Hunt

My treasure hunt began with a Bible study class many years ago. I have always enjoyed studying the Word of God; but because I was very quiet, I had no idea that I would one day be teaching the Word. I attended a Bible study where the teacher was pregnant and ready to go on maternity leave. One Sunday she came to me and said that when she went on leave, God wanted me to take over the class. I laughed! You must understand that even though I was always prepared, I hardly spoke. If I were asked a question, I would answer, but I was not going to elaborate or give additional information. I was quiet, or so I thought. Here is the challenge with which I was faced. After praying and asking God for direction, this thought came to me—was I going to allow my quietness and fear to keep me from discovering a potential destiny that God might have in mind for me? Or, was I going to step out in faith and believe that God would give me what I needed at the exact moment I needed it so that I could fulfill His calling on my life?

I went on a treasure hunt to remind myself about the things I enjoyed when I was a child and a young adult. I remember when I was a child I had often spoken at various church and school programs. I was always singing (believe me I am no singer) and leading other kids around in various activities. It was then I realized that I had allowed the enemy to steal my voice and silence me. In later years, I came to understand that my quietness was not my natural state of being and was never intended to be. The enemy did not want me to share the Word of God with others, and I had allowed him to silence me. I decided that it was time to be free and accepted the charge of teaching the Bible study class. God did much through that one act of obedience, even though fear was crouching at my door.

Accepting the Call

The Lord had said to Abram, "Leave your country, your people and your father's household and go to the land I will show you. I will make you into a great nation and I will bless you; I will make your name great, and you will be a blessing. I will bless those who bless you, and whoever curses you I will curse; and all peoples on earth will be blessed through you." So Abram left, as the Lord had told him; and Lot went with him. Abram was seventy-five years old when he set out from Haran.
Genesis 12:1–4 (NIV)

God called Abram and told him to leave his family and his country. Abram was living in a pagan country, but God stepped in and interrupted the path he was on. When God called and Abram accepted, God changed his name from Abram, which meant "exalted father," to Abraham "father of many nations." Why is this significant? The name change signified a change in his destiny. Abraham was seventy-five years old when God called him, and he had not yet produced an heir. God was giving him a clue as to what was planned for his destiny and this new adventure God was taking him on. God was about to bless his life with the heir that had been missing for seventy-five years. God planned to give Abraham a son through whom he would produce children as numerous as the sand on the seashore and the stars in the sky. Only God could take his childless state and turn it into a miracle. When he accepted the call, God did not immediately tell him where he was going. Abraham had to step out in faith, believing that he was hearing the true and living God.

When God calls, you must be willing to obey and step out in faith even though you may not understand where the road will lead. This obedience to His will demands movement; and movement requires trust—trust in God, which will get you to the desired destination God has for your life. Like Abraham, you must be willing to accept where God leads because He will order your steps to the right destination. I challenge you to step out in faith. Believe that you are hearing God and begin the movement that will deposit you on the road to fulfilling His destiny for your life.

Discussion and Reflection

Life Application:

1. Embrace the fact that God has called you to fulfill great things for Him.
2. Know that many are called. Accept your calling.

Challenge:

1. Determine to fully embrace all that God has called you to do.
2. Don't let anyone or anything stop you from fulfilling your calling.

Discussion Questions:

1. What dreams has God called you to fulfill?
2. How can you discover these dreams?
3. Where should you begin your treasure hunt?
4. What treasures are hidden in you?
5. How do you accept the call to dream?

2. WHY HAS GOD CALLED YOU?

GOD HAS CALLED YOU for various reasons. God called you before He formed and designed your life and placed you in your mother's womb. During your formation, He impregnated you with hidden treasures for you to use to fulfill His destiny. God had intimate, as well as foreknowledge of who you were before He placed you in the womb. He knew you to such a degree that He determined which parents would be suitable for you. God planned your race, and He is not surprised about where you begin your destiny. He planned the location of your birth and decided that it would be a good starting point to train and prepare you for your calling. He also planned the members of your family.

Have you ever wondered what God was thinking when He placed you in the family in which you were raised? Know that He made no mistakes in your placement; and God uses everything you have ever dealt with, whether good or bad, in the fulfillment of your destiny. All that life has handed you can be used to fulfill your purpose when you place yourself in the creative, loving, and powerful hands of God. God will not waste a single moment of the trials you have endured *if you are willing* to submit them to Him. He will work it all out for your good and turn what was meant for evil in your life into something meaningful (Romans 8:28). He will use all of it to fulfill His dreams in you just as He used all the tragic situations in Joseph's life to fulfill his dreams. Joseph's story demonstrates how God is constantly working in your situation even when you can't trace His hands.

Called To Dream

Joseph, a young man of seventeen, was tending the flocks with his brothers, the sons of Bilhah and the sons of Zilpah, his father's wives, and he brought their father a bad report about them. Now Israel (Jacob) loved Joseph more than any of his other sons, because he had been born to him in his old age; and he made a richly ornamented robe for him. When his brothers saw that their father loved him more than any of them, they hated him and could not speak a kind word to him. Genesis 37:2–4 (NIV)

I love the story of Joseph the dreamer. Here was a young man who knew how to dream and believed in dreams. His very name meant, "May God add," so it is evident that he was always looking to God to add more to his life. Joseph was a favored son, and this favoritism caused jealousy among his brothers. His brothers hated him because he found favor with his father. Then it appeared he found favor with God because God began to speak to him about dreams and destiny. He was only seventeen years old and did not yet understand that he should not share his dreams and visions with just anyone.

What Joseph and so many of us have discovered is that often people will not rejoice with us about the things God is speaking and revealing to our hearts about our destiny. In his dream, Joseph saw his brothers bowing down before him, and then he saw eleven stars and the sun and moon bowing down before him. The eleven stars represented the other eleven tribes of Israel, while the sun and moon represented his father and mother. His brothers wanted to kill him but were unable to do so. When God places dreams and visions in your heart, the enemy cannot destroy you because those dreams and visions must be fulfilled. That statement should boost your confidence to know that whatever difficulty you face if you stay connected to God, your destiny will keep you and your dream alive until its fulfillment.

The sharing of his dreams, the favoritism by his father, and the purpose God had for his life caused Joseph to be sold into slavery. God used this season in his life to process his heart and life and to prepare him for the fulfillment of his destiny. The enemy attempted to silence his dreams, but God turned it around and used the difficult situation in Joseph's favor.

Though called to fulfill a great destiny, Joseph began a journey that would lead him away from his family, his familiar support base, and to find himself alone with only God for support in a foreign country. Even if Joseph may not have recognized it, while he was away from home, he was aligned with the best source of help that could be found anywhere in the world. God became Joseph's ever-present help in his times of trouble, and he faced many troubled times (Psalm 46:1).

The enemy tried to seduce him while he served as a slave in his master's house, but he refused to get involved in the devil's plan. He rejected the enemy and chose God's plans instead, which landed him in prison. Joseph served thirteen years in prison, a place he did not deserve to be in, for a crime he did not commit. He ended up in prison for his God-given dream, his calling, his righteous stand, his integrity, and his love and obedience to God.

God, indeed, called him and had a plan for his life; but it was clear that God had also allowed Him to walk down this road to the fulfillment of his dreams. If you are wondering if every call from God will land you in prison or something equally devastating, be assured that whatever God calls you to do; He gives you ample grace to accomplish it no matter where the road may lead you. Despite Joseph's tribulations, God accomplished amazing things in his life, and He will do the same in yours.

Unlocking Your Dream

Have you ever had a dream or vision that you cast aside? You cast it aside because you thought it had no value or because someone caused you to believe that God no longer speaks through dreams and visions. I encourage you to get a hold of those dreams again. God still speaks to you in dreams and visions as He did with Joseph all those centuries ago. The dreams He has given to you can be manifested and realized, if, like Joseph, you believe, embrace, and trust God for the total fulfillment of them in His time.

I believe God gives many of you dreams at night because during the day you are so busy, and your mind is so active that sometimes He cannot get specific directions to you in the way He would like. He speaks to you in your dreams while your spirit, soul, mind, and body are resting, and you are not disturbed. God will not shout over the loud noises that are in your life. Often the TV is on, someone is yelling or talking loudly, and the phone is ringing—no wonder you can't hear Him clearly. Many of you wonder why you hardly hear from God, and you question why He does not speak to you as often as He does to others. I can assure you that God speaks to you regularly, but the noises in your life drown out His voice. Your busyness also keeps you from quiet time spent with Him where He desires to speak to you either in your spirit or through His Word. God is intent on reaching those He has called to do work in His Kingdom, and He will use any means available to get you to the place where you fix your attention on Him. God has dreams and plans that He has called and selected you to fulfill. I encourage you to practice turning off the television, radio, and every other noise source, so you can get the revelation of this great dream God has for your life.

Ask yourself this question, "Am I so busy that God has to speak to me in night dreams, so He can get me to the place He has called and destined me to be?" I know, like me, you love and appreciate a Father who will go to any lengths for His children; but I challenge you as I challenge myself, be open to God speaking to you while you are either asleep or awake because when He speaks it will be for your greater good. Many years ago, I was extremely busy at work and involved in everything at church with never a moment to call my own. I was busy for God (or so I thought), since I was doing a lot of work in the church and potentially fulfilling my dream. I got into my car one day after, yet another meeting and this song was playing. The words by the songwriter Larnell Harris are simple:

I miss My time with you, those moments together. I want to be with you each day, but you hurt Me when you say you're too busy, busy trying to serve Me. But how can you serve Me when your spirit is empty? There is a longing in My heart for wanting more than just a part of you, it's true. I miss My time with you.

I had to pull into a parking lot and grab a tissue. That simple song clearly depicted that in all my activity, even though most of it was in service to the Lord, there was no replacement for time spent with God. It was a lesson to me that God wanted more than just my service. He wanted me. God used a song to deliver a message that He had attempted to deliver for a long time, but in my busy and hurried life, I simply did not hear Him. Know that God's best, His dreams that He planned for you to fulfill, are waiting for you if you would slow down, quiet yourself, and begin listening for His still, small voice and His ever-present instructions. God is ready to make His deposit of a life-changing dream into your life. Are you willing to do whatever is necessary to hear Him?

Sanctified for God's Use

If a man therefore purge himself from these, he shall be a vessel unto honor, sanctified, and meet for the master's use, and prepared unto every good work.
II Timothy 2:21 (KJV)

The word "sanctified" tells me that you are set apart and made holy for use by God. Does it make you wonder if you are qualified to run this race to your destiny? Relax and take a deep breath, this word means to be blessed of God. God has called and blessed you to be used by Him in the way He chooses. God has washed and purified you from the inside out, so you look like Him and can reflect Him to all those you meet (Psalm 51:7). II Timothy says that you are to turn away from unrighteousness; and, in doing so, you could be special bowls of gold and silver that could be purified and used by God for good works in His Kingdom. In sanctifying you, God has chosen, separated, declared, and sealed you as belonging to Him. This sanctification is a progressive transformation of every believer into the image of Christ. It is a process in which you continue to turn away from wrong and embrace that which is true and right. God purifies you and begins the process of making you morally fit. Sanctification is part of the redemptive work of Christ through the working of the Holy Spirit, who indwells every believer.

Think about a time in your life when you felt free, accepted, loved, pure, and satisfied. Do you have that time in your mind?

When God sanctified you, He freed you to be accepted in His beloved Presence. In His Presence, you experience such satisfaction that you know there is absolutely no way that you can fail because He is backing you every step of the way.

God has sanctified you so that you can accomplish the great calling He alone placed in your heart. Your calling is to fulfill His plans for your life in the earthly realm. When you believe and embrace this, you will experience life at its fullest and understand God always intended you to live your life fully satisfied.

Rejoice in the fact that God has sanctified you to be used by Him and for His purposes. I think about the priests in many of the world's religions. Many of them have chosen to be set apart for service to God and, in many ways, to be secluded into that service. I am happy to announce today that without going into seclusion you can be equally as sanctified, equally as set apart, and you can do it in freedom by choosing to follow completely after God in every decision and in every way that He desires. Each day you make the choice whether to live sanctified and set apart for God. Each decision you make will solidify that choice.

You must determine in your heart that Jesus is not just your Savior; but make Him your Lord, as well. What do I mean by this? When you receive Christ in your heart, He becomes your Savior; and you will spend all of eternity with Him. For Him to become Lord of your life means that you totally surrender your plans and will over to Him. You allow Him to govern every decision you make whether small or great. You don't make a move without consulting Him. In this way, He becomes Lord over all of your life because you acknowledge that without Him you can do absolutely nothing. As you live out this concept, He will daily, weekly, monthly, and yearly become Lord over more and more of you until He has all of you.

The Preferred Choice

But God demonstrates his own love for us in this: While we were still sinners, Christ died for us.
Romans 5:8 (NIV)

Do you know that you are God's preferred choice? Go ahead and say it. "I am God's preferred choice." The passage above is clear about the love God has for you. While you were still in sin, God sent Christ to die for you. Consider the fact that this preferential treatment is how God has chosen to demonstrate His great love and forgiveness toward you. Through the death of His Son, He forever revealed that you are His preferred choice. He demonstrated His preference by adopting you into His family. God took a fancy to you and chose to make you His own.

As I reflect on my own life, I think about some of my choices. I think about the relationships that I have formed, the friendships that I have had in my life, the places I went to school, and the list goes on. My point is, in life, you have made many choices because they were your preference. Something about them spoke loud and clear to your heart, your emotions, and your desires. You chose, as you felt led, often because something or someone answered a great need in your heart that you were not aware was there. God adopted you because of His preference for you. He did so because you were open and receptive when He called. You chose to hear and obey His voice; and when you did, He spoke to your heart saying, *"You are the preferred one for Me."*

In the story of the birth of Jesus, God called Mary and she responded with a heartfelt decision that simply said, "Here I am Lord, use me." That simple decision made her the preferred choice. Do not make the mistake of thinking if Mary had said "No," that God would have stopped there. God would have kept calling until the right person responded because He had to redeem us back into a right relationship with Him. His ultimate goal was not just Mary saying "Yes." His plan was much bigger than hers. His plan was for the salvation of mankind. Mary was a willing vessel and became one of God's preferred children in the earth. When she said "Yes" to her calling, she began a life-altering journey that would change the course of her life and world history.

The same holds true for you. When God calls, you must make a simple decision to answer and obey. God will then begin the process of making you into one of His preferred children. His goal is to use your life to bring Him glory. In His service, you will find fullness of life and joy; but along this journey, you will also encounter some difficulties. The difficulties and challenges you encounter are often for your development. Before God completes you, often you must be broken so that the Potter can remold you into His shape and design for your life. He desires to mold you into a perfect reflection of Himself. When this molding is complete and other people see you, you will reflect Him so clearly and sincerely that they themselves will answer Him when He calls out to them.

Called to Worship

Yet a time is coming and has now come when the true worshipers will worship the Father in spirit and truth, for they are the kind of worshipers that the Father seeks.
John 4:23 (NIV)

You were created, called, and designed to worship God. He called you to demonstrate His praises throughout the whole world. The Father seeks after true believers, those with hearts set on Him, who are neither ashamed nor afraid to give Him their highest worship. Worship is your calling; therefore, you must have a heart to get into the Presence of God regularly, to adore, reverence, and lift Him up. Worship is deep intimacy with God. It is allowing God to look into your heart as you pour your life out to Him. And it is also seeing the love, the forgiveness, and the mercy that fills His heart for you. In worship, you kneel in the presence of the one and only King, as you pay Him homage. You demonstrate your humility and your awe of His greatness and His amazing goodness.

As you worship God, it takes your focus off your concerns and yourself and places it on the One who can provide a way of escape from your difficulties. When you worship God, you will discover that He desires to give you a future filled with hope and blessings (Jeremiah 29:11–12). He wants to prosper you, so that you can know what a loving, tender, and caring Father He is.

This great love that the Father has for you is a part of your heritage as His son or daughter. When Lucifer, the former praise and worship leader, decided centuries ago that he wanted to be like the Most High God and ascend to God's throne, God kicked him out of heaven, along with one-third of the angels who rebelled with him (Isaiah 14:12–15). You were designed to take his place in worshiping God by giving God your heart, love, reverence, praise, and worship. You worship God in Lucifer's place. Every time you lift your voice to shower God with the admiration He deserves, God comes in and sits down in the midst of your praises. As you adore Him and stand in awe of His vastness, God is tickled because here is a person who adores and reveres Him as the one and only God. This person truly understands that He is forever deserving of all praise.

He called you to worship Him because of His great love for you and because He wanted you for His very own. As you come to

Him, He begins the process of transforming you into His image and likeness. Just as you enjoy family life on earth, God desires a family of His own. He desires a family that will praise, worship, and adore Him. As you worship Him, He lavishes you with His goodness, His blessings, and His many great rewards. He is a Father who adores His children and wants the very best for them. Consider your children, when they honor and obey you, do you not desire to shower them with all that you have? I wonder where that idea came from? Since you are made in the likeness of your Father, you have His mind on everything you do in your life.

Discussion and Reflection

Life Application:

1. Understand that you are called by God to fulfill a great destiny.
2. God has sanctified you for use in His Kingdom.

Challenge:

1. Go on a treasure hunt and find out why God has called you.
2. Embrace that calling.

Discussion Questions:

1. How do you know that God has called you?
2. What has God personally called you to do?
3. How do you answer His call?
4. Why does God prefer you?
5. Now that you are called, what should you be doing?

GOD HAS CHOSEN YOU FOR A SPECIFIC PURPOSE

∿

"God has chosen you because He wants you for His very own.
He desires to live through you, so you can experience amazing
fullness and completeness in your life."

Joan E. Murray, Author

3. CHOSEN BY GOD

~

JUST SAYING THE WORD *chosen* makes me feel special, how about you? You are special to God—so special that He gave His best gift in the form of His Son to die for you. So special that even if you were the only person on earth, He still would have sent Jesus to die just for you. That is truly special!

When God chose you, He selected you from a group. In essence, He specifically handpicked, gathered, and selected you to be with Him. God desires a relationship with you that is far above all other relationships you will ever have. He chose and adopted you to be His very own.

We are Adopted

He predestined us to be adopted as His sons through Jesus Christ, in accordance with His pleasure and will - to the praise of His glorious grace, which He has freely given us in the One He loves.
Ephesians 1:5–6 (NIV)

I cannot talk about your being adopted without talking about the adoption of the Son of God. Have you ever considered the fact that Jesus was adopted? Sure, He was! He was the Son of God by the Virgin Mary, but Joseph, Mary's earthly husband, had to receive instructions from an Angel of the Lord to take Mary as his wife when she was found to be pregnant and to raise Jesus as his own earthly son. Those of you, who are adopted, consider what great company you keep. Jesus had an earthly father in Joseph, who loved Him, provided for Him, and helped raise Him to fulfill His great destiny. In previous centuries, it was a known fact that when a child was adopted, he or she received all the same benefits as a natural-born son or daughter. And, in those days, although a natural-born son could be disinherited, a son by adoption *could never* be. This is great news for you who have been adopted by God, you cannot be disinherited!

As a result of the birth of Jesus Christ, His adoption, death, and resurrection, you have been adopted into the family of God. You are now legal heirs to the inheritance which God has laid up for you through Christ. Adoption speaks of a wholehearted love for another that will cause one to take ownership and responsibility for that other person's life. That is precisely what God has done for you since Adam and Eve sinned and plunged you into bondage.

When God adopted you, He embraced and brought you into fellowship with Him. He assumed total and complete responsibility for you; and in doing so, He provided a home, a place of rest, hope, and safety for you. You are adopted because you are so loved by God. The depth of that love ensured that God would never leave you alone in your sins and sorrows. His love would not leave you comfortless, in pain, and without hope. He went to a cruel death on the cross to redeem you.

Like Jesus and so many of you, a stepmother adopted me. Part of being adopted when you are older is being able to make the proper adjustment into a new home and a new environment. Sometimes these transitions can be easy and other times they can be difficult. Even in the difficult moments, you must understand that none of it is a surprise to God. He knew what family you would be adopted into, and He planned to use your experiences from that family to form character in you. He uses all your experiences to fulfill the destiny that He has chosen for you. Remember, you can rise above any circumstance you face because you are never alone. God's presence is with you wherever you go.

Chosen by Love

For God so loved the world, that He gave His only begotten Son, that whosoever believeth in Him should not perish, but have everlasting life.
John 3:16 (KJV)

It was love that sent Jesus to a horrible cross. It was love that had Him beaten and carrying a cross to Golgotha's hill. It was love that kept Him on that cross when He could have stepped down at any time. Love caused Him to accept the beatings and the piercing of the sword in His sides. Love sent Him into Satan's domain to get the keys of death and hell back from him—love, love, love for you and me. Are you getting the picture? Love would not stop giving until you were redeemed.

When God calls out to humanity, it is a call filled with love for the people whom He is seeking. There are people who are listening and waiting to hear this voice of love. In *John* 10:4–5 & 27, *God says, His people know His voice and a stranger's voice they will not follow.* They know the voice of love. When God summons you, you hear and respond to that summons because it is filled with love. By your heartfelt decision to hear His voice and follow Him, God chooses to use you for His purposes. There are many of you whose hearts are tender, open, and filled with love for God and who dearly desire to please Him. That is the reason why you are His "chosen ones," because you made a willing and willful decision to be His chosen vessel. In essence, what you have done is simply chosen the One who first chose you.

He chose you out of love, and He provides for you out of love. God has chosen you to demonstrate His praises to the whole world. You do so when you show people that you are not ashamed to love and adore Him. For those of you who have often wondered why God created you, let me answer that question for you ... *He created you out of love, to worship, praise, and adore Him.* He has called each of you out of the darkness you were born into to live in His marvelous, radiant light. He desires that you understand the fullness of who He is to you. Know that there was no price too great that His love for you was not willing to pay.

Let me take that even a step further, there was no depth too low that He was not willing to go to for you. He chose the cross, and He went into the pits of hell to redeem you back to Himself.

God has chosen you because He wants you for His very own. He desires to live through you, so you can experience amazing fullness and completeness in your life. He wants to fill your life with His blessings and His goodness so that you overflow with joy and peace. His love for you is measureless and without boundaries. While you were yet a sinner, love in the form of His Son was dying for you.

Chosen to Follow

So Abram left, as the Lord had told him; and Lot went with him. Abram was seventy-five years old when he set out from Haran. He took his wife Sarai, his nephew Lot, all the possessions they had accumulated and the people they had acquired in Haran, and they set out for the land of Canaan, and they arrived there.
Genesis 12:4–5 (NIV)

When God chose Abraham, it was at the time in his life when his father, Terah, had died. God called him into his destiny when there was no further allegiance to his earthly father or ties to his former way of life. Abraham and his family lived in a pagan land where the people served pagan gods, so God had to remove him from that environment to get him into his destiny. The scripture tells us that the eyes of God are searching the earth, looking for people whose hearts are perfect and sincere towards Him (2 Chronicles 16:9). This does not mean that God is looking for people who will never make mistakes.

Just like many men and women in the Bible, you will make mistakes from time to time and that is the reason grace has been given to you. These mistakes do not disqualify you from service in the Kingdom of God. God is looking for people whose hearts are ripe, open, and willing to follow Him. God saw in Abraham a man who would respond to His call and obey His instructions. God is looking for the same things in you. Are you willing to be used by God? Then you must be like Abraham and make a choice to walk away from your familiar surroundings so that you can hear and obey the instructions that God wants to impart to you.

Abraham's obedience to God was the key to his success, blessing, and prosperity. He willingly walked away from family, friends, houses, and land to follow God. I am sure that he had great opposition from those who did not understand what he was doing and his desire to move away from them. You will face opposition when you decide to walk away from close associations, jobs, relationships, and financial blessings to walk into the things God has reserved for you. Like Abraham, whatever you give up, God will eventually return to you one hundredfold. The result of Abraham's obedience was his total faith in God, the generations of people he fathered, and a history full of amazing blessings from God. We will talk further about the way God changed his life, as we journey through this book.

Here is a challenge for you! What do you desire God to do in your life? Is it worth the sacrifice to seek and follow Him with your whole heart? Can you trust that what He plans for you is far greater than anything you are currently experiencing? You must believe that His plans will unfold great wonders and fulfillment for you. Take the plunge, be like Abraham, and make a decision that you are not willing to settle where you are, and that you want to go on the adventure of a lifetime with God. I assure you that it will be an adventure. Abraham did not know where God was leading him, he just started walking, listening for God's instructions, and trusting that he was hearing God's voice. You must take your first step of faith, and God will indeed show up and give you instructions about where to go and what to do when you get there.

Chosen by a Dream

Joseph had a dream, and when he told it to his brothers, they hated him all the more. He said to them, "Listen to this dream I had: We were binding sheaves of grain out in the field when suddenly my sheaf rose and stood upright, while your sheaves gathered around mine and bowed down to it." His brothers said to Him, "Do you intend to reign over us? Will you actually rule us?" And they hated him all the more because of his dream and what he had said. Then he had another dream, and he told it to his brothers. "Listen," he said, "I had another dream, and this time the sun and moon and eleven stars were bowing down to me."
Genesis 37:5–9 (NIV)

When God chose Joseph, He saw in Joseph a man who would believe in dreams, embrace them, and realize that they had value. He found a man who, even while he was at his lowest, would still receive and interpret dreams, and continue to serve and glorify Him while in the very pit of his life. While in prison, Joseph did not stop using his gift of dream interpretation. He continued to dream and to interpret dreams for others. He served people while in the most miserable seasons of his own life. He saw the needs of the hurting, the confused, the sad, and the broken around him, and he could not turn them away when they came to him with their dreams. Joseph took time, even in his own disappointments, to lift others. God surrounded him with dreams to be interpreted so that God could sharpen and hone his skills in preparation for when he would be used in a greater way.

He interpreted dreams for Pharaoh's cupbearer and baker. The cupbearer's dream had a happy ending. He was restored to his position in the king's house, but the baker's dream ended in disaster for him since he was killed. When the dreams were fulfilled as Joseph prophesied, I am sure that God used that as a marker in his life to let him know that the dreams, which had been placed in his own heart, would one day also come to pass. Joseph was learning to lead people while he was confined.

When God chose Joseph for this difficult path and assignment, He saw a man who would have extreme trust and confidence in Him. He knew that when Joseph was tried and tested in the fires of adversity, he would come out as pure gold. God knew that about Joseph because He formed him to be just like Himself. Even though Joseph may not have had this knowledge about himself prior to the testing, God had faith in him that he would walk out of this situation victorious. His choice in Joseph would mean life or death to nations including the children of Israel, a people chosen by God. Famine would have wiped them out without Joseph's dream; his obedience to God; his willingness to demonstrate faith in God, and his trust and belief that he was indeed hearing from God.

The adversities you face will also test your faith, belief, trust, and commitment. You will get to see what you are really made of as you are plunged into the pits of life. Your character will be tested, tried, and formed during these difficult seasons; and your integrity level will also be tested to its limit. Often you don't know what is in you until you are put through testing, but God is fully aware of what is in you. Whatever is in you, good or bad, will rise like cream to the surface when pressure is applied to it. Pressure will squeeze out of you the good intentions of your heart or the bad intentions.

Have you ever been in a relationship where you wanted to truly know the person, so you prayed that God would reveal their character to you? I have prayed such a prayer, but in doing so, I was not expecting the pain I would experience from the revelation. I learned that people would lie to you; lie about you, and also attempt to damage you to make themself, feel better when they are under severe pressure. When God does this unveiling for you, He does it so you will be able to make an accurate decision about the relationships you choose. You have a choice to make about continuing or terminating the relationship based on what God reveals. God is such a loving Father that you will never be able to say that He did not warn you when you made choices in your life that brought you pain. If you are willing to listen and obey Him, God will give you instructions every time, just like he did to Joseph.

No matter the difficulties you face, you must face them with confidence as Joseph did. Trust that God will be there to see you through every trial you face because He promised to never leave you nor forsake you. The love of God and His dreams for you are without limits, and that is the reason He has chosen you for Himself. He has chosen you to be a part of His family. Take the limits of God and take the limits off yourself because nothing and no one can stop you from dreaming and succeeding but you.

Discussion and Reflection

Life Application:

1. Welcome and embrace the fact that God has chosen you for a great purpose in Him.
2. You are adopted by God to be a part of His family.

Challenge:

1. Decide to be one of the chosen ones.
2. Allow God to develop and use you for His highest purpose.

Discussion Questions:

1. How do you know that God has chosen you?
2. What did God have in mind when He chose you?
3. What convinced God to choose you?
4. How do you serve the One who has chosen you?
5. Now that you are chosen what should you be doing?

4. REST FOR THE CHOSEN

~

IN CHOOSING YOU, GOD desires not only to use you but also to give you rest from your own labor and striving. When God declared the oath in His anger, He was talking to the Israelites. He made them a promise to give them rest after leaving Egypt, where they had spent many years in hardship doing labor-intensive work. God wanted to give them rest from their labors, their efforts, and from doing things in their own strength. He had a plan to give them "true rest." To experience this true rest, His people had to learn how to fully trust and rely on Him. Part of this rest was to believe that He had great plans and provisions for their lives. This rest was a "rest of faith."

A Rest of Faith

"Come to me, all you who are weary and burdened, and I will give you rest. Take my yoke upon you and learn from me, for I am gentle and

humble in heart, and you will find rest for your souls. For my yoke is
easy and my burden is light."
Matthew 11:28–30 (NIV)

It is clear from the scripture that God desires to give you the same rest He planned for the children of Israel. He knows that you have been wearied by the struggles in your life. He knows the burdens and responsibilities that have been laid on you, and He wants to replace these heavy burdens with His yoke, which is easy. He wants to deliver you from all the things that have kept you down. Often, these burdens are sorrowful; and you can experience a feeling of doom and gloom as you struggle with the weight of them. That is why He wants you to experience this *rest of faith.* In this *rest of faith,* you will come to know God. You will develop such faith in Him that you always understand that He will bless you abundantly and use you for His purpose and His glory. As you rest in faith, you will no longer have to worry, be in despair, or let anxiety rob your heart from resting. You will come to know that God can be trusted to bring about many blessings and provisions for your life.

The Israelites had struggled for so long that they had a difficult time accepting the rest, which God was attempting to give them. They continued to do things in their own strength and might. They were fearful and not able to trust God to deliver them. Fear led them to make one bad decision after another. They sinned constantly, and a loving God could not reach them with the rest He so desired to give them. When God declared this oath that they would "never enter His rest," I get a picture of God throwing His hands up in the air in desperation because they were just not getting it. They were missing the fact that He longed for them to receive what He promised, but they could neither hear Him nor receive it. God did not make this oath because He did not want to bless them, but because they simply would not receive His blessings.

How many times do you think God has thrown His hands up in the air because you have also refused this *rest of faith?* He has attempted to reveal this great plan of rest for you, but to no avail. God wants to do for you what He planned to do for the Israelites, which is to give you "true rest." His rest for you is a rest from worrying about things that you cannot change. I know, like myself, many of you have worried about the bills you have difficulty paying or the sickness that doesn't seem to go away even after you have prayed and prayed. Many of you have worried about the losses you have endured. I can tell you today that worry does not make anything happen faster or make it easier for you to get the results you desire.

One day it dawned on me that worry is a sin and that each time I worry I am saying to God, "You are unable to help me." Imagine me telling the Creator of the Universe that He does not have what it takes to bail me out of my difficulties. My worry says to God, "I don't trust You to make a difference at all in this situation, and You are neither big enough nor great enough to handle it and to deliver me." I have found that the things I worry about, ninety-two percent of the time never materialize. I have wasted energy, time, and health worrying about something that may never happen, instead of trusting God who loves me enough to make it all better.

As you learn to rest in God, to believe and trust Him, you will come to know that He is in your personal struggles with you and that He will help you to overcome every fear you encounter. His plan and destiny for you will manifest fully and completely in your life as you let go of fear and embrace faith. As you rest in Him, sometimes you will find yourself in what I call the "waiting rooms" of life. In these waiting rooms, God will allow circumstances to happen so that you can face yourself; and, as you begin to deal with yourself, He will begin to form His character in you. When you experience lack or drought, it is a test of your faith level. You and I are not exempt from difficulties if we expect God to use us at all in His Kingdom. You must look to Jesus when you begin to question why. Though sinless, He paid a heavy penalty for you. For God to use Him, Jesus went through His own waiting room where pressure was applied to Him to see what would come out of His heart. That is why the Bible says, *"He is touched with the feeling of our infirmities"* (Heb. 4:15). He fully understands your struggles and has demonstrated the way for you to overcome them. You overcome by trusting God and believing what He has promised you. He is faithful to accomplish great things in your life even though you may have to wait and struggle a bit.

One of the things you will come to understand, as you wait on God, is that His chosen ones must be equipped for His highest purpose and that equipping comes with a cost. When God planted His desires for you into your heart, He knew that you would choose to obey and serve Him. He had foreknowledge that you would choose His desires over your own, and in doing so you would choose to go through the difficult times of testing.

My Test

Over the years, I must admit that I have worried, cried, and prayed to be released from many of the tests and trials that I faced. I did not want to go through the pain of waiting for or even trusting in God. I wanted God to do what He was going to do and do it now. I had not accepted or embraced God's rest of faith. I did not know what true rest was, and today I am still learning to rest and trust in Him. During one of the many tests I tried to get out of and bypass, God stopped me and asked me a question. It went something like this, "When you were in school and failed a test, what happened?" Since I knew this was leading somewhere and was unsure if I was ready to follow, I was slow to respond. I said, "Well, I guess I had to take the test over again." Come on, it was not a guess; I either took the test over or failed the class and would not advance any further. God proceeded to remind me that if I failed a test or a class, the teacher would not advance me to the next grade. He then said, "What makes you believe that if you keep failing these tests in your life, I will promote you to the next level in Me?" Ponder that for a moment.

He went on to say, "If earthly men know that they cannot advance you to the next level in school while failing, He who created these laws and principles would most assuredly not advance you to the next level in Him." I had only one choice, I would either go through my difficulties without murmuring and complaining or even asking "Why me," or I would later be required to take the same test again because it would surely come back in a different form.

Many times, I have had to dig my heels in, set my face as flint, and rest in God, knowing that in the middle of these difficult seasons, He was right there with me. He promised to never leave me to face them alone (Heb. 13:5). I continuously seek Him to teach me how to truly experience this *rest of faith* that He wants to give me, so I can enjoy each day of my life. I have found that when I am not resting, trusting, and believing Him, it is hard to enjoy each day that He gives me.

God's *rest of faith* is a benefit to you, who embrace the truth, that He does not want you to attempt to do things your way, in your own abilities, or your own strength but to truly trust Him. He will provide the answer, the resources, and the help you need to accomplish great things in your life. Embrace His *rest of faith* and allow Him to do in you what only He can do.

Discussion and Reflection

Life Application:

1. God wants you to find true rest in Him.
2. God plans for you to enjoy the provisions that can be found by faith in Him.

Challenge:

1. Learn to rest in God by trusting Him.
2. Have confidence that God will do all that He has purposed for your life.

Discussion Questions:

1. How can you experience the *rest of faith* God has in store for you?
2. What is keeping you from experiencing God's true rest?
3. Why do you worry?
4. What are the results in your life when you worry?
5. How can you free yourself from this habit of worrying?

DISCOVERING WHO YOU ARE!

~

"Each of you must go on an adventure to discover who you are and why you are so special. You must also search for the reason God created you to be who you are."

Joan E. Murray, Author

5. WHO ARE YOU?

~

NOW THAT YOU UNDERSTAND that you are called and chosen by God, it is time to focus on who you are and the position and authority you have in Him. I have discovered that *not* many of us have a true understanding of who we are, why we were created, and how to truly live our lives to the fullest. As previously stated, you have been called and chosen by God to accomplish great things with your life. To fully understand and walk out that calling, you must get to know who you are.

To answer the question "Who are you?" I am going to take you on a journey through the scriptures. In *Genesis,* when God created you, He made some great statements about who you are and what you have been created to do. On the sixth day of creation, God finalized the creation of man and there was a decision made in heaven by God the Father, God the Son, and God the Holy Spirit. He said, "Let us make man in Our image and after Our likeness." I call this conversation "the ultimate meeting."

The Image of God

"God is a Spirit, and His worshipers must worship Him in spirit and in truth."
John 4:24 (NIV)

You were created in the exact image of the Father, Son, and Holy Spirit. You look like the Father your Creator; therefore, you have been given His creative abilities. God spoke and by His spoken words the earth began to bloom, the fish began to swim, the birds began to soar, and the creatures on earth began to spring to life. You have been given the same creative abilities with your words. You can speak into existence exactly what you want in your life, and by your spoken words, you can create and bring into existence a destiny filled with amazing wonders. As Spirit, God does not have the same form that you have. He is therefore looking for the invisible part of you, your spirit man, who was created in His image to join in worship with the true Spirit, who is God. You have creative abilities that you have not yet tapped into. The more time you spend with God getting to know Him intimately, the more His creative abilities will come alive in you.

When God designed and created you in His image, you were given "God consciousness," which gave you awareness before you were saved that something vital was missing from your life. In your soul, you have a conscience, which helps you to know what is true and right and gives you the ability to reason these things out. Your spirit has been given the same God-consciousness, which enables you to hear the voice of God and to respond to Him when He speaks.

God gave you power to rule over the fish of the sea, the birds of the air, and over every moving thing upon the earth. God gave you two kinds of power, "Dunamis," which is the Greek word that in the English language means, "Dynamite." You have explosive strength and ability to accomplish what you are assigned to do. Then God gave you "Katros," which is the Greek word that means "ruling power." God has given you the ability to rule, govern, and reign in this life. You have been given everything you need to be a conqueror. I want you to know that when God reviewed everything He had created, He declared that it was "very good." Make no mistake about it, God knows that as His creation, you have been designed with great qualities for a life that can be spectacular, and He expects to showcase His abilities in and through you.

The Image of Jesus

In the beginning was the Word, and the Word was with God, and the Word was God. He was with God in the beginning.
John 1:1–2 (NIV)

Jesus Christ the Son, the sacrificed one, was in the very beginning with God. He was the spoken Word that God sent to His children after four hundred years of silence when no one heard from God between the Old Testament book of Malachi and the New Testament book of Matthew. During those four hundred years, the children of Israel did not receive any instructions from God. God sent His Son; and in John 1, He was called the *Word*. He came as the *Word* because they had been missing a word from God for years since God had become silent in their midst. God promised to send help; and He sent His Son, the *Word*, who willingly gave up His life for you. The life of Jesus was that of a giver. He gave all He had for you, and in turn, He has given you the ability to be a giver willing to give your all to those who are in need. This need you have to give is an indication that you are being transformed into His image.

The Image of the Holy Spirit

But you will receive power when the Holy Spirit comes on you; and you will be my witnesses in Jerusalem, and in all Judea and Samaria, and to the ends of the earth.
Acts 1:8 (NIV)

The Holy Spirit is the breath of life, and He causes things that are dead to live. He breathed into you the breath of life, and He is the enforcer of God's will and plans in your life and in the earthly realm. Because of His power living in you, you can also breathe life into your dead situations and see them bloom back to life. It is the Holy Spirit's presence in your life that enables you to make the right choices and decisions. He is always in the process of developing your character because it is His job to transform you into the image of the Son of God. As you listen and obey His commands, you daily grow to know Him intimately. This level of intimacy will help you to reflect the love of God to everyone you meet. He gives you the power to share the love of God with those who are lost and alone.

Worshipper of God

To be a worshipper is the key to how much you will experience God, discover who you are, and fulfill this great destiny that He created for you. As a worshipper, you worship God the Father, God the Son, and God the Holy Spirit. For those of you who may be wondering why I have separated them with such emphasis since they are one, I did so because often time we like to focus on one of the three instead of understanding that, though they are One, they are three distinct persons with different functions, as defined earlier in this chapter. You worship because God devised a plan of redemption for you when Adam and Eve sinned and fell from grace. He did not let you live out eternity in pain, grief, and suffering. You were designed to worship because of His Son's life given so freely for you. You could have suffered the consequences of your own sins; but you were released from its penalty because of the victory of Jesus over death, hell, and the grave. You no longer must fear death because the sting of death has been removed for the believer. 1 Corinthians 15:55 says, "O death, where is your sting, O grave, where is your victory?" The fear of death has been removed from us because Jesus took that power back from the devil. I love the scripture in II Corinthians 5:8 which says, "*Absent from the body is to be present with the Lord.*" It is very clear that you will be absent from the body one moment and the very next moment you are in the presence of God. No struggle, no fear, and no waiting. That is what the death of Jesus accomplished for you.

Part of the reason you worship is because of Jesus' continuous intercession for you. Have you ever been concerned whether anyone is praying for you? Let me shout it to you today, "*Yes, someone who understands you completely is in the presence of God, day and night talking to God about your condition.*" Jesus is seeking the mercy of God on your behalf. He asks God to pardon your sin every time you mess up and miss the mark. He is the only one in heaven and earth worthy to stand before God for you because He is the sinless, spotless, Lamb of God. He has total and complete access to God, plus He has God's full attention.

You worship God because you love Him not only for all the wonderful things, He has done for you, even though that is a blessing; but you worship Him primarily because He is your One and only God. Psalm 95:6 says, "Come let us worship and bow down, let us kneel before the Lord our maker." This is a picture of a life that is surrendered and submitted to the will of God. Worship says to God, "There is no more I, only You." It is going all the way with God even in your seasons of lack, fear, and doubt. Worshipping God means that you are willing and ready to bow your knees in total respect, adoration, reverence, and honor to God. It speaks of a life that will not hold anything back in a desire to let God know how much you appreciate and thank Him for not leaving you alone or comfortless when you had no other refuge but Him. Worship says, "I am in awe of You and wonder at Your unfailing love for me, and why You have given it so freely to someone so undeserving." You are a worshipper because you understand that the One you worship, will come into your presence to receive the praise and adoration that you are so willing to lavish on Him each time you lift your voice to Him. You should live to worship.

Heirs of God

So you are no longer a slave, but a son; and since you are a Son of God,
God has made you also an heir.
Galatians 4:7 (NIV)

Now if we are children, then we are heirs—heirs of God and co-heirs
with Christ.
Romans 8:17a (NIV)

I want to begin by defining the word "heirs," because I want you to get a clear understanding of what an heir is. Heirs are beneficiaries of a kingdom, which means that as the heirs of God, you have a kingdom reserved for you in heaven. While He was here on earth, Jesus made it plain that He was going to prepare a place for you, so that when you get there all will be ready. I believe the place that has been reserved for you is filled with the many things you now enjoy in your life. God has prepared it for you with love and abundance so that as His child, you can enjoy the benefits of being His.

As an heir, you are inheritors of all the promises made to you by God in His Word. You are in line to receive blessings that are reserved for those who love the Lord and call upon His name. Throughout His Word, God has promised you a legacy, as He did for Abraham and Joseph, and many other men and women in the Bible. You have a heritage in God because you are sons and daughters of His. He has specifically designed you to receive everything that He promised for your life. I think about how some earthly parents often work to leave a legacy, an inheritance, for their children. God is the ultimate parent after whom your parents were modeled; and they learned this principle from a loving Father, God Himself. They learned that God has provisions in store for all His children, so they modeled what has already taken place in heaven by leaving you an earthly legacy.

As a son or daughter of God, you must follow the leading of the Holy Spirit because the Word promises that He will only lead you in truth. As you follow His leading, He will lead you to the provisions God has reserved for His heirs. When I speak about following the leading of the Holy Spirit, I am speaking about following the promptings of the "still small voice" that speaks quietly to your spirit. You know that He is speaking to you when you have any uneasiness about moving ahead with your plans. When you are uneasy about any decision, wait on God. You also know that He has not given you clearance when you decide, and you experience no peace with that decision.

As an heir of God, He will not leave you to make decisions on your own because He promised to lead and guide you in every area of your life. So, while you are here on earth, God wants to lead you to the many blessings and provisions He has for you; and He will lead you by the Presence of the Holy Spirit. Why is the Holy Spirit so vital in your everyday life and in every decision? Because He is the very Power that raised Jesus from the dead, and He knows every path you will take and whether the path will lead to blessings or destruction in your life. With the Holy Spirit living in you, He has sealed you as a child of God, and He will lead you by the peace you experience when you decide. Let the peace of God be your umpire for every decision you make.

As an heir, you have intimacy with God and you must come to know Him as "Abba," which means daddy or father. This level of intimacy means that you have spent time with Him and know what He will do in most situations. It also means that you have direct access to Him because you have spent quality time with Him and know His mind and His thoughts. Time spent in prayer talking with God on a regular basis will develop this level of intimacy. Time spent reading His written Word will also give you insight into the character and nature of God. In addition, time spent fellowshipping with other believers will help to deepen the relationship. As you begin to share what He has done and is doing in you, you will begin to sharpen one another and cause each other to grow and develop in the things of God.

One of the benefits of being a son or daughter of God is that you are no longer slaves to doubt and fear. Doubt and fear no longer have the same stronghold over your life. You come to a place of knowing that the greater One lives in you, and He gives you the power to overcome. "God has conferred sonship on you," this means He has placed His stamp of approval on you and marked you as His son or daughter. When others look at you, they will see a difference because you radiate the image of the One you were created to look like. As sons and daughters, you represent a King who provides for you, who showcases His blessings through you, and who demonstrates His consistent love and grace toward you. When others see you, they see a reflection of His glory and an absolute assurance of His Presence in your life.

As an heir of God, you are joint-heirs with Jesus because He is the first-born son; and therefore, everything He owns you own. Think about that for a minute—everything Jesus owns you own. The Word tells us that everything has been put under His control, and He owns and governs it all (Phil. 2:10–11). As a joint heir with Him, everything has been put under your control, and you also own and govern it all. As an heir of God, you have rights and privileges that you have not yet begun to tap into. There is healing in your words and your touch. When you love people with the love of God, this also brings healing to their lives.

As an heir, you have victory over every circumstance because your victory was accomplished on the cross at Calvary. All you need to do is believe it and act like it. This will keep the enemy from harassing you because he will realize that you know who you are and whose you are, and you understand the power you have been given over him. You have been blessed and no one can curse you. You have the authority to nullify every negative word that has been spoken over you, as you use the Name and apply the Blood of Jesus. When you declare what is right and true, everything you say will be recorded in heaven and in hell.

God created you to be the head and not the tail, which means you were created to be looking down from a position of strength, not to be crawling around on your hands and knees, looking up to others from a position of weakness and lacking authority. Remember, I told you at the beginning of this chapter that you have been given dynamite and ruling power over all things. Now is the time for you to rise, take your place, and begin to act like the One in whose image you were created. You are destined for greatness in Him, and you will fulfill every destiny He has placed before you because the greater One lives in you. You have the same power that has been given to your elder brother and co-heir, Jesus Christ. I challenge you to believe it, receive it, and begin to act like it. Know that through the death of Jesus, you have been made an heir of God and joint-heir with Jesus Christ.

Discussion and Reflection

Life Application:

1. God has made you in His image so you look like Him.
2. You are important in the Kingdom of God.

Challenge:

1. Dare to be different and embrace who you are.
2. Walk, talk, and live as the heir you are.

Discussion Questions:

1. Who does God say you are?
2. What are your rights as an heir of God and joint-heir with Christ?
3. What is your level of authority?
4. How do you embrace who you are?
5. How do you receive and enjoy your inheritance?

6. YOU ARE SPECIAL!

~

DO YOU LOVE TO hear that you are special? Does it cause you to lift your head a little higher, push your shoulders back, and walk as if you have a destination in mind? You are indeed special because you are special to God. One of the things I often say and you will probably hear it repeated time and again as you read this book is this: "If you were the only person on earth, God would still have sent Jesus to die for you because that is how special you are to Him." I want you to take a moment and ponder that statement; and while pondering it, consider that it takes a special person to win the heart of God. He specifically created you because you are special to Him.

I think about the fact that scientists say that there are millions of sperms that approach the female egg for a child to be born. Consider that out of those millions, you were the one who made it; you were the one specifically hand-selected by God to be born. This is a great moment to stop and say, "Thank you, Lord." Acknowledge that He chose you Himself to do great things for

Him; and in doing so, you can enjoy a life filled with blessings and contentment. To be special means that you are distinct and unique in your makeup. God has created you as an original. You don't look like anyone else, talk like anyone else, or have the same personality or makeup as anyone else. You are exceptional to God, and you are exclusively designed for Him. Let me try to define God. God is a specialist who only deals in rare and beautiful treasures, so He was specific in His choice of you. When God created you, He concentrated only on your design. He was not trying to design others at the same time He was designing you, so they would end up looking like you. He made no carbon copy or replica of you. He focused exclusively on you, and He went into great detail in your design. To say you are special does not cover the amazing work of art that you are. There is not another person like you on the planet. Your footprints and your hand prints are different from every other person God created. Have you noticed that there is not a single person who sounds like you? You are a masterpiece created in Christ Jesus for good works. Celebrate your uniqueness and know how special you are to God.

The Discovery

Each of you must go on an adventure to discover who you are and why you are so special. You must also search for the reason God created you to be who you are. In my discovery, I must admit that God had to do a lot of correcting and re-affirming. Here is why. Like me, many of you do not always like what you find, as you begin to get to know yourself. Let me begin with the fact that I would look in the mirror and always find fault with myself. My skin was not as blemish-free as I would like for it to be. My size was not the right size; I could be a little taller. How about this one, couldn't God have made me more intelligent? Why is it that I don't get the same breaks or blessings as others? Does God care about them more than He does me? Let me stop here because this list could go on and on, you know how it is? One day, I was headed on this downhill spiral when God decided that enough was enough and He needed to intervene before I ended up in depression with no way out. He said to me, and I quote, "Joan, every time you look in the mirror and criticize something about yourself, you are saying to Me that I made a mistake in the way I formed and designed you. You are saying to the King, the Creator of this beautiful universe, that He made a mistake and did not know what He was doing with your formation."

Imagine my surprise and remorse as I hurriedly stammered and told God that was not exactly what I meant. As I repented, I asked Him to help me appreciate everything about myself and why He created me as I was. Over time, I began to experience a deeper level of His love and approval. This love and approval were always there, but I was not focused on them, I was only focused on what I termed "my flaws." I want you to go on a discovery of your own. What are some of the things you have been telling God about yourself? Remember, He knew exactly what He was doing when He created you. You are not a surprise to Him, and you are definitely not a disappointment. He loves you just as you are! You are a masterpiece. That being said, please know that there are areas in your life God wants you to work on. You must impact your heart with His Word so that you look like Him. You must exercise and eat right, so that He dwells in a temple that represents Him well to the world. Take care of the things that you can; and with those you cannot handle, ask God for His help. He is a present help for you with whatever you need.

A Royal Priesthood

But you are a chosen people, a royal priesthood. 1 Peter 2:9a (NIV)

The Bible declares that you are a royal priesthood. The word royal means that you are regal in your appearance, and you stand out in a crowd of people. You are princely in your nature and disposition because He who resides in you is a King. You have a stature that is magnificent because you are of the Royal family, the family of God, and through His lineage, you have been given nobility. As a priest, our example is the High Priest Jesus.

Therefore, since we have a great high priest who has gone through the heavens, Jesus the Son of God, let us hold firmly to the faith we profess. For we do not have a high priest who is unable to sympathize with our weaknesses, but we have one who has been tempted in every way, just as we are—yet was without sin.
Hebrews 4:14–15 (NIV)

In the Old Testament, a high priest was the one who was consecrated to the Lord. In the New Testament, a high priest is referred to as one who is holy, consecrated, and divine in nature. Jesus is your true High Priest because He represents you before God. The scriptures declare that all other high priests have been abolished in Him because He offered Himself once and for all as the final and ultimate sacrifice for your sins. His death on the cross and His sacrifice can never be repeated. The shed blood of Jesus provides a way for you to share in His priestly activities. The New Testament clearly teaches the priesthood of all believers. (1 Peter 2:5 - You also, like living stones, are being built into a spiritual house to be a holy priesthood, offering spiritual sacrifices acceptable to God through Jesus Christ.)

You now share in Christ's priestly activities. Each time you share the Word of God with someone, you are acting as a priest in the Kingdom of God. When you bring people into a relationship with Jesus Christ, you introduce them to the great High Priest. Jesus as your great High Priest holds the highest position of authority there is in heaven and on earth. He understands your weaknesses and your failures because He was indeed tempted like you are, yet without sin. Jesus suffered the greatest suffering anyone ever endured; and He keeps right on giving to you and taking care of your concerns, worries, and failures. The Bible compares Jesus your High Priest with one other, Melchizedek, who was the king of Salem in the Old Testament. The Bible defines Him as a priest of the Most-High God and as the king of righteousness and peace. He was without a father and mother and had no beginning of days or end of life. Like Jesus, Melchizedek is forever known as a true high priest.

As your High Priest, Jesus is your guarantee of a better covenant. In this covenant relationship, you can boldly enter His presence and petition Him about your needs. I want you to know that a covenant is very different from a promise. Where you may easily break promises, covenants cannot be broken. A covenant is completely binding on both parties. In the Old Testament, the shedding of blood often sealed covenants. As your High Priest, and because of the shedding of His blood, Jesus can completely save all those who come to Him. This is the covenant of salvation that you have with your great High Priest. As your High Priest, Jesus is holy, blameless, pure, set apart from sin, and He has covenanted with you to meet your daily needs.

As part of His Royal Family, you have rights and privileges that ensure your success. When Jesus declared on the cross "It is finished," He forever took care of anything that would hinder you from walking fully in the promises and provisions that He provided for you. You are royalty from a royal bloodline, which has no beginning and no ending. As royalty, there is a kingdom reserved for you. Say it to yourself: "I am royalty, I am from a royal bloodline, and there is a kingdom reserved for me." I encourage you to say it until you believe it and begin to act like you believe it. Whatever you practice doing on a regular basis will eventually become a part of you. Live like you not only believe that you are from a royal family and a royal bloodline but that you know and understand that it is the absolute truth.

A Holy Nation

But you are a chosen people, a royal priesthood, a holy nation...
I Peter 2:9a (NIV)

When God calls us a holy nation of people, He is talking about a group of people He has consecrated for Himself. You are blessed because God has given you His blessings. The Bible encourages you to be holy as He is holy (I Peter 1:16). This means you have the privilege of living a holy life with the help of Jesus. To be holy is to know that you are separated and set aside to be of special use in the service of God. It was because of the holiness of God, and us being separated from Him by sin that Jesus had to die to redeem us. God's holiness would not allow Him to fellowship with us because we would not be able to stay alive in His presence.

The Bible teaches that light and darkness cannot co-exist together. God is light, and we were living in darkness, so the two could not meet until the blood of Jesus washed, cleansed, and purified us. Throughout the Bible, the word holiness is used to define the character of God. The word holy means to be saintly, sacred, and pure; and it defines the loving nature of God. It means that God is separate from evil. God personifies holiness in all His attributes, and He calls you to live a life of holiness. When Jesus walked the earth, evil spirits recognized Him as being holy because He is the Son of God with God's nature.

When Jesus promised that He would send someone to live in us to be our comforter, He came in the form of the Holy Spirit. It is not surprising that His name is "Holy." Let me use some creative license here. The Holy Spirit wears the name "Holy" as a badge that causes you to recognize the very nature of the One who lives on the inside of you. This Holy One gives you the ability to live a holy, separated, and consecrated life unto Him. He ensures that you will be godly in your character and that you will exemplify a life of godliness to others. As a holy nation, we are a people who form a community. This community is made up of believers who understand we are from an unknown country and are only temporary dwellers in this land. As a result, we do not settle in as if we have no other destination because there is a place reserved for us. It is a place where we will rule and reign because God has decreed it to be so. Second Timothy 2:11-12 says, "*If we died with Him, we will also live with Him. If we endure, we will also reign with Him.*"

The book of Revelation tells us that we will be priests of God and Christ and will reign with Him for a thousand years (Rev. 20:6b). Revelation goes on to say there will be no more night and that we will not need the light of a lamp or the light of the sun, for the Lord God will give us light and we will reign with him forever and ever (Rev.22:5). Believers who persevere through life's many trials, who overcome and endure to the end, will one day reign with Christ and be a part of His administration (Rev.2:26). Not only has God called you to reign with Him, when He returns, He has also given you authority to rule and reign now. Genesis 1 gives you a clear picture that He has placed all things under your control. You have authority over the fish of the sea, the birds of the air, over the livestock, and over all the earth and the creatures that roam upon the face of the earth. A loving God has made provision for your present and future.

As the holy nation of God, you are from a commonwealth and from one tribe, the tribe of God. You are a people created by one God, called by one God, chosen by one God, and given life by the same God. The picture is clear God selected each of you to make up His Kingdom and connected you as one nation. You are a nation of rulers with authority to rule and govern this whole earth.

A Peculiar People

Who gave Himself for us to redeem us from all wickedness and to purify
for Himself a people that are His very own, eager to do what is good.
Titus 2:14 (NIV)

Has anyone ever called you strange or unusual? So many of us have been called strange and unusual. Understand this is a compliment. God has called you His peculiar people. You are His peculiar treasures. To the world and those who do not know Christ, you are strange and unusual. What they see is someone who belongs exclusively to a God who has distinguished you in your nature and character from them. What they consider unnatural in you is the natural order of things in the Kingdom of God. As a believer, God has asked you to live a life set apart, which means you must wait until marriage to be intimate, you give when you are in need, and you sacrifice yourself to be a blessing to others because that is the nature of the One you serve.

The world lives on a reverse system from yours, which is why they think you are strange and peculiar. When the world defines you as strange and peculiar, what they are saying is that you are a marvel to behold. They cannot understand you. You confound their logical way of thinking because you do not act like you should when you are tried in the fires of adversity. It is hard for them to comprehend that you can rejoice even in the death of a loved one. They do not know the One who sustains you with His peace during this crisis. They do not have the understanding that because your loved one was a believer in Jesus Christ, just as you are, one day you will spend all of eternity with them. So, when you choose to rejoice even during your tears and grief, they consider you to be strange and unusual. Celebrate your odd makeup by understanding that those who live in the light of Christ fully understand you, and you are unique and special to those who matter.

You Are a Giver

For God so loved the world, that He gave His only begotten Son, that whosoever believeth in Him should not perish, but have everlasting life.
John 3:16 (KJV)

For He hath made Him to be sin for us, who knew no sin; that we might be made the righteousness of God in Him.
2 Corinthians 5:21 (KJV)

And being found in fashion as a man, he humbled himself, and became obedient unto death, even the death of the cross.
Philippians 2:8 (KJV)

But God demonstrates His own love for us in this: While we were still sinners Christ died for us.
Romans 5:8 (NIV)

I included the above scriptures to give you a taste of why you are a giver. The One you serve is a giver who keeps giving to you without fail. Because of His great love, He cannot stop giving to His children. You were not only designed to look like Him but also to act like Him. You cannot help but give because you have His nature. Reflect on the number of times that you have given just because someone was in need. Even though you might not have had much, you simply could not walk away without helping. Have you ever emptied your cupboards or refrigerator because you learned someone did not have food? How about planting a finan-cial seed because someone did not have gas to get to his or her destination?

The scriptures are clear that because of love, God gave. While you were alone, lost, and away from Him, God was planning your redemption. He was looking for a way to give His best to you. It is unnatural as a believer for you not to have a giving heart. You can give of your time, your effort, your resources, and yourself. I can tell you for sure, that when I am giving, I am fulfilled. When I step out of self, and meet the needs of others, is when I feel that I am fulfilling my life's purpose.

There are people who live to give. They live in your homes, on the mission fields, in your churches and communities. You are one of those people. Giving is an act of favor that you show to someone in need. It is stepping in and meeting a need because you understand that God has blessed you not only to meet your own needs but also to help others. If you choose to become a vessel that God uses in His Kingdom to meet the needs of others, you have a guarantee that whatever leaves your hands will always leave a residue of blessings in your life. There is no way you can give unless God has first given to you. Every time God blesses you, He does this so you will be blessed, as well as be a blessing to others.

I remember a time when I had very little resources but was giving and giving until I had nothing left. I went to God with my complaint. My complaint went something like this: "God, I am giving and giving, and I have given all that I have with nothing left over to meet my needs, what is the problem?" God's clear response to me was, "You are to give, but I never asked you to give everything, leaving nothing to take care of your responsibilities." He took me back to the book of Malachi where He only told me to bring my tithes and offerings to the storehouse. He made it clear that in my giving I should always seek Him first for direction because He always provides enough to meet my daily needs after I have presented Him with my tithes and offerings. I have learned to seek God for direction when I feel a desire to plant additional seeds in the life of His people and in His Kingdom's work.

You are a giver by nature because of Him who lives in you. You are exactly as He planned and designed you. When you give, you reflect Him to others, and you are also able to see that you are growing to look just like Him. Live to give and watch God overflow you with His abundance.

Discussion and Reflection

Life Application:

1. Believe that you are special to God.
2. Realize that He has a mansion reserved with your name on it.

Challenge:

1. Choose to have the nature of Jesus Christ.
2. Choose to be a giver.

Discussion Questions:

1. What does living holy mean to you?
2. How do you live a consecrated, set-apart life?
3. What makes you different from the world?
4. How do you develop the traits of a giver?
5. Why is it important that you give?

SERVING IS YOUR HIGHEST CALLING

～

"Your heart is the center of your being and your innermost self. It is the source from which you serve."

Joan E. Murray, Author

7. CALLED AND CHOSEN FOR SERVICE

~

THE REASON YOU OFTEN see success in certain industries is because of the service they provide to meet the needs of the people. You are a people who provide service to others; and, in doing so, you are able to realize great personal success. Service is providing aid to someone with a need. It is to be helpful and useful in your daily life. When you serve, you are performing a duty to others; and often it is a duty they cannot provide for themselves. For you to serve, you must want to serve. One of the requirements is that you serve with your whole heart. This means that you pour yourself totally into whatever the task so it will be a success. The way you give your best in service is to remember that when you serve, you are serving as unto the Lord and not men. Although men receive the blessings of your best service to the Lord, God will reward you for your service and the good deeds you perform for others.

The Power to Serve

So He got up from the meal, took off His outer clothing, and wrapped a towel around His waist. After that, He poured water into a basin and began to wash His disciples' feet, drying them with the towel that was wrapped around Him.
John 13:4–5 (NIV)

Jesus demonstrated for you what service looks like. He, the Son of God, did not consider it beneath Him to provide an act of service by washing His disciples' dusty and dirty feet. In this act of service, Jesus left you an example you must emulate as you choose to serve Him. Part of your service to God is your wholehearted commitment to His plan for your life. His plan is for you to carry out His service in the lives of the people you will encounter. God has not only provided you with what is necessary for this service, but He has equipped you with everything you need to serve Him and others.

To serve with power, humility must be a part of your life. Without humility, you will not be able to give yourself away unselfishly. What do I mean by giving yourself away? Every time you choose to serve, you choose to set yourself aside to meet the needs of others. It is unnatural to deny yourself to take care of someone else's needs. It takes power and humility to submit your pride, your ego, and your own desires to say, "Yes, I am available for whatever you need." This power comes through a relationship with Jesus. In this relationship, you learn that whatever position you find yourself in, you are not limited to that position because it is a place where God is being formed in you more and more. This formation will raise you to great heights and new levels in Him. Jesus, knowing that He was the disciples' Savior, had no hesitation in stooping down and serving the very disciples who would serve Him with their lives after He ascended back to heaven. In essence,

He first served the ones who would in turn give their lives in service to Him. He is your model of servanthood as you journey through life.

Heart of a Servant

Your heart is the center of your being and your innermost self. It is the source from which you serve. It has nothing to do with your external makeup; but, when your heart is good and right, that goodness can be seen and felt by all. The Bible says that out of your heart flow the issues of life (Prov. 4:23). Servanthood is a heart condition. Whatever begins in your heart will eventually overflow into all areas of your life. If you purpose in your heart to serve others, it will eventually become a natural part of your makeup. As a servant of God, you are committed to the things of God and to what He has assigned you to accomplish. Because of this commitment, you can be trusted with responsibilities to serve; and you should perform each act of service at the highest level.

As you serve others, you must serve them with humility. Humility says that you will submit to others and follow their instructions. A person with humility always demonstrates modesty in service. They do not allow vanity to keep them from accomplishing the goals they have set for themselves. No project is too large, too small, or insignificant for them to tackle. A servant with a heart of humility is one with courage, who is unafraid and unashamed to appear small in the eyes of the world in his or her desire to be of service to God and others. A person with a servant's heart gladly receives assignments, serves with a glad heart, and is willing to be led by the Spirit of God.

In our society, it appears as though someone who does menial work is not successful. But is that really so? Each of you have a service you must perform, and every service you give benefits someone else. Without the garbage man, your neighborhoods would be dumps. Without those who cook, clean, and provide the help you need, you would not be successful in what you endeavor to do. Service is the responsibility of everyone; and whether you are serving in a large or small capacity, you are engaged in taking care of the needs of others. Examine your heart to see if you have patterned yourself after Christ's example of servanthood. It is in the giving of yourself and in a willingness to serve others that you find not only your true calling in life but true contentment as well.

Requirements for Service

Therefore, I urge you, brothers, in view of God's mercy, to offer your bodies as living sacrifices, holy and pleasing to God this is your spiritual act of worship. Do not conform any longer to the pattern of this world, but be transformed by the renewing of your mind. Then you will be able to test and approve what God's will is His good, pleasing and perfect will. Romans 12:1–2 (NIV)

For every service that you offer, there will always be some requirement for you to fulfill. The same holds true for the service you provide in the Kingdom of God. One of the requirements for serving is that you must willingly offer yourself to God as an act of worship. Your body, your very person, must be given up as a willing sacrifice to the desires of a Holy God. Another requirement is that you willingly let go of the conformity to the world's standards and fully embrace the standards of His Kingdom. You are required to be unmoved by what the world thinks about you, but you are to be more concerned with what God thinks of you.

I have discovered that we spend a lot of time pleasing others, and we will never be able to please everyone. Here is the key. If you work at pleasing God, as you please Him, all others will eventually come in alignment with Him. Some of you have focused for so long on pleasing people that you have often missed the opportunity to please God. As you work to please God, you are required to renew your mind with His Word daily; and in doing this, you will come to an understanding of God's pleasing and perfect will for your life. The Bible encourages you to be mindful about not thinking of yourself more highly than you ought (Rom. 12:3). Instead, consider others and be quick to please them, oftentimes putting them first. This is sacrificial giving where you lay down your desires to meet the needs of someone else.

You are encouraged not to think too importantly of yourself, but to clothe yourself with humility, so that you will not get ahead of God. Many of you have been given talents and abilities by God. It is vital that you do not think too confidently about your talents and abilities but realize that God gave them to you. These talents and abilities have been given to you as part of the requirement for your service to others. As you begin to meditate on what God requires of you, be sensible, reasonable, and rational in your thinking. Keeping these things in mind will keep your life in balance and in proper order. Realize that your gifts are given to you as part of your service. Do not covet another person's gift because their gift may seem more important to you than the one you were given. Cheerfully use whatever gift God has given to you. That gift is what God will bless and cause to work successfully in your life. He will not bless the use of someone else's gift that you may be trying to copy. Remember, He did not create you as a copy, but as an original. In doing so, He has placed the gifts in you that will best fulfill your service to Him.

Another requirement for service is that you must know and accept your limitations. Know what you are called and destined to do and stop trying to do what you were not called to do. Often you will take on tasks because it appears that no one else is stepping up to the plate to do them. If you learn how to wait on God, He will always provide what is needed, when it is needed. The reason you do not see more of His provision is because you get ahead of

Him and the people, He has reserved to help you. When these people arrive ready to provide the help, there is no room for them and nothing for them to do because you have already filled the slot. God created a body of believers with many parts, and He requires that we serve together as one (Rom. 12:4). The book of Psalms declares that where there is unity there is strength and God commands a blessing (Ps. 133). His blessings are commanded when you are unified, when you fulfill the requirements for your life, and when you make room for others to do what is required of them. You must only do what God has specifically asked and assigned you to do with your time and your life.

Discussion and Reflection

Life Application:

1. Understand that service is your highest calling.
2. Service is your rightful position.

Challenge:

1. Make serving others a way of life for you.
2. Do not consider yourself too good to serve.

Discussion Questions:

1. How do you know if you have the heart of a servant?
2. Do you walk in humility toward others?
3. Are you willing to offer yourself in service to God?
4. How often do you seek to please others instead of God?
5. Why is it important that you seek to please God first?

8. SERVE GENEROUSLY

~

WHEN PEOPLE VIEW SERVICE, it is either viewed from a positive or a negative mindset. Serving is not a subservient position. You have been called to serve. In the earthly ministry of Jesus, He provided service to His disciples and us when He died on the cross to redeem us. The Son of God did not consider it beneath Himself to reach down and help those in need. God has called and chosen you to serve others with the same degree of love and compassion. There is a principle that is well known and used in the Kingdom of God; and it is, "If you give it will be given to you. A good measure, pressed down, shaken together, and running over, will be poured into your lap. For with the measure you use, it will be measured to you" (Luke 6:38). When you give your best in service to others, you will in turn reap only the best.

Everything you give is a seed. Each seed you plant will fall into either good or bad soil. When a seed enters the soil it will germinate, grow, and then bear fruit. Each time you serve others you are planting seeds that will generate a harvest in your life. To serve generously, you must learn to give from your heart. It is difficult to give your best seed if it is not coming from a heart that desires to give into the lives of others. If you are serving reluctantly, then the question must be asked, *"Are you truly serving?"*

I cannot begin to tell you the number of times I have provided service or help to someone, and my heart was not fully involved or engaged. I often did it because there was a need and no one else was available to fill it. Though the service was given, it was not given with joy or with a spirit of cheerfulness. In retrospect, I have evaluated many of those times and come to the realization that, though the help was given, those receiving the help would have benefited so much more if I had given with joy and cheerfulness. It would have felt less like an obligation and more like my calling if I had chosen to serve generously.

Whenever you step outside of yourself to serve others, God will cause His favor to abound in your life. When you serve, you must serve as if you are serving the Lord. Ultimately, any rewards you receive come from Him. Your God is such a generous God that He will supply you with all you need as you develop a heart for service. When you serve others with generosity, it is a demonstration of your heartfelt thanks to God for all He has done and will continue to do in your life. When men see your generosity to others, they will know that it is God-inspired and God-given, which in turn will enable them to praise Him for the work He is doing in and through you. When you serve the poor and the needy with all that you have, scripture promises that God will ensure that your righteousness endures forever.

Wholehearted Service

When I consider wholehearted service, the word integrity comes to mind. Integrity is giving your all to whatever you have been called and chosen to do. It is the assurance others have that they can depend on you to keep your word. To wholeheartedly serve others, you must have total commitment to the process. This commitment must be such, that if you are unable to meet the obligation, you will call the person and state the reason that you are unavailable. When you serve the Lord wholeheartedly, you are then able to transfer that wholehearted service to those He places in your life to bless. All your heart must become engaged and involved in your service. For every assignment that you receive, you must be willing to pour yourself into it until it overflows with God's presence.

You will face times of uncertainty as you begin to give your all, but you must remember that courage will get you into a position for God to use you. It takes courage to do what seems impossible to you, but nothing is impossible with your God. If God has given you the assignment, He has also given you the grace to accomplish it. God will not ask you to do something that He has not already equipped you to do. You may be unaware of the equipping; but, as you take a step of faith—for some it will be a leap of faith, you will discover that what you needed was already in you just waiting to be discovered.

In your service to others, you must keep in mind that you are formed with different traits and personalities. There are some people who are soft-spoken, others who speak slowly, and still others who move at a slower pace. They require time and understanding when you are serving them. Have you ever been on the phone with someone who was taking a long time to explain what they needed? I have been in situations like that and have started to tap on the desk and get anxious for them to get to the point. God will often use these times as lessons for me. He reminds me that in serving others, I must accommodate who they are, and be willing and available to meet their needs, even if they take all day to state it. Remember, that you are working as unto the Lord when you are serving others. He will give you the grace to do everything that He has assigned your hands to do.

The Sacrifice of Service

We put no stumbling block in anyone's path so that our ministry will not be discredited. Rather, as servants of God we commend ourselves in every way: in great endurance; in troubles, hardships, and distresses; in beatings, imprisonments and riots; in hard work, sleepless nights and hunger; in purity, understanding, patience and kindness; in the Holy Spirit and in sincere love.
II Corinthians 6:3–6 (NIV)

The Apostle Paul gives us a clear understanding of the cost that he and others endured, as they provided service to others for the cause of Christ. Hard work is a requirement for doing anything great either in the Kingdom of God or with your life. All of you at times must sacrifice something, whether it is your time, efforts, or some friendships, as you pursue what God has destined for your life. I think about people who start new businesses. They spend countless hours in the preparation process as well as the time spent to provide the actual service. It costs them something to develop a successful business, but they are willing to make sacrifices to meet the needs.

When you decide to do something of great value with your life, you must approach it with the understanding that this is a life-long commitment and responsibility. Often the preparation process will be labor-intensive, and you may have to endure some struggles to get to the result. In this sacrifice, you must give total dedication to what you are doing for it to produce the results that you are seeking. At times you must crucify your flesh and your personal desires to get to the desired destination.

In any endeavor you consider pursuing, you have to prepare

for disappointments. Disappointments are setbacks that will keep many from accomplishing their goals. These disappointments can be a painful time in the process, but they do not have to linger in your life. You must learn to get up, dust yourself off, and get back to the task at hand. As you continue this journey, you must pursue it with all your might by pushing disappointments aside and not letting them keep you from your destination.

Part of the sacrifice that many of you have paid, or will pay, is that you have to push yourself beyond your own limitations and what you think is possible for you. You must push yourself beyond your limits and discover that there is so much more you have to give. All of you will come to the realization that a *time sacrifice* is a requirement to getting your destiny fulfilled. This *time sacrifice* can sometimes deplete your strength if it is not properly balanced and maintained. As you serve, you are dependent on others to provide you with assistance; and, when they fail to do so, you will experience some heartbreaks and setbacks, which will require even more of your time.

When you choose to go the distance in your sacrifice of service, you will discover that it can be lonely because many people do not understand or agree with your commitment, your dedication, and your sacrifice. You must solidify in your heart the reason you are determined to serve with such generosity and sacrifice. The key is this: whatever you do from your heart and give in the spirit of love will always be returned to you. You cannot out give God.

The Rewards of Service

And without faith it is impossible to please God, because anyone who comes to Him must believe that He exists and that He rewards those who earnestly seek Him.
Hebrews 11:6 (NIV)

There is a reward not only for your faith but also for your service. Since God is the rewarder of those who seek after Him, He is also the rewarder of those who will provide service to others. Your faith is the key that unlocks your storehouse of blessings, and that same faith brings pleasure to the heart of God. He is pleased with you when you demonstrate confidence and trust in Him. You must believe that God exists for you to serve Him wholeheartedly. At some point in your relationship with God, you must get beyond the point of just believing in Him, to a place of knowing that He is real and available to you. As you earnestly seek after Him, He comes with His rewards to your life. God is no respecter of persons. Wherever He finds faith, He rewards. If you take the principles of God's Word, embrace them, believe, and apply them, they will work in your life even as God has allowed them to work in the lives of others. God is not partial. He will not bless one and not another who is applying the same principles of His Word in their life.

As you pursue God and the rewards that come with Him, you must determine to do what pleases Him because it is your greatest desire to please His heart. You must get to a place in your life where you seek after God with such zeal and passion that you exhaust yourself in the search. I think about many couples I have known. While they were in pursuit of their spouses, they were extremely determined and would stop at nothing to win their attention. They would exhaust themselves in the pursuit because they understood that the reward at the end would be worth it. The reward of pursuing after God is well worth all the effort, prayer, time, and commitment you put into it. He will not only fill up every empty space in your life, but He will overflow your life with Himself, His goodness, and His blessings. The story of Hannah gives clear insight into what zeal for God can produce in your life.

Hannah's Story

In 1 Samuel chapter one, we find the story of Elkanah, Hannah, and Peninnah. Elkanah married both Hannah and Peninnah, but he loved Hannah more. Hannah was often sad and tearful in spite of all the love she received because she could not have children and give Elkanah heirs. Peninnah, on the other hand, was very fruitful and produced many children. She provoked and taunted Hannah constantly about her barrenness. This went on year after year. When they went to the temple to offer their yearly sacrifice, Elkanah would give Hannah a double portion because of his love for her, but it was just not enough. Consider that centuries ago, unlike today, women were mocked and scorned for not having children and people believed it was a curse from God. In the bitterness of her soul, Hannah went to the temple of God where she wept and prayed to the Lord. She went to the one person who could deliver her. In her desperation, she promised God that if He gave her a son, she would give him back to Him all the days of his life. As she wept and prayed in the temple in the early morning hours, Eli the Priest thought she was drunk and rebuked her. She told him that she was not a wicked woman, but one who was anguished in her soul and was pouring out her heart to God. He then blessed her and said, "May the God of Israel grant you what you have asked of Him."

She left the temple and went home, and the Lord remembered her and gave her a son. She named him Samuel saying, "Because I asked the Lord for him." She kept the baby at home until he was weaned. Then honoring her covenant with God, she took the child to Eli the Priest, and left him in Eli's care. Hannah was extremely desperate in her need for a child. God allowed her to wait for such a long time that she was willing to do whatever God wanted her to do to get this son. God used her desperation and need to give her a son whom He would use for His highest purpose to bring Him great glory.

God had already planned a great destiny for Samuel, but He had to prepare Hannah's heart so that she would willingly give him back to God for His purpose. As Samuel grew, God was with him and eventually Eli died, and Samuel became a priest in his place.

When Hannah pursued God, she received the reward of her pursuit and the answer to her prayers. I want you to take hold of this picture. For years she was mocked, scorned, and taunted. She wept and prayed for God to deliver her. God moved in her situation by rewarding her with a son. In turn, God used this longed-for son to be the Prophet to the Israeli people. Now each time Hannah, Elkanah's family, and the Israeli people went to the temple to present their yearly sacrifice, they were ministered to by none other than Hannah's son. The son she sought God for earnestly. When the people heard the name "Samuel," they could not help but remember that this was Hannah's, the barren woman's, son. God not only gave her a son, but He gave her one who was famous, one who had His heart and was a leader in His nation.

Consider all the mothers who had children during Hannah's time. Their children have died and gone to their rewards and today there is no mention of them in the Bible. However, the son Hannah prayed and waited for with such anguish, we are still hearing and learning about today. God is, indeed, a rewarder of those who diligently seek Him. God gave Hannah additional children who were a blessing to her life, but their names are not mentioned in the scriptures. When you wait and earnestly seek God, He will bless you and showcase your blessings for the entire world to see and remember how great He is.

God is perfecting you for service in His Kingdom. He is looking for people who are ripe, mature, and complete in Him.

People who will not stop after providing a little service but will press into Him to do more and more. God's eyes are searching for people with hearts that are ready to receive an outpouring from Him, so they can do great exploits on the earth. He is looking for people who will be found faithful until the end of their days. God is looking for you! There are tremendous rewards in your service to God and to others.

Discussion and Reflection

Life Application:

1. Generosity comes from the heart.
2. You are called to serve others with generosity.

Challenge:

1. Do not allow distractions as you begin your service.
2. Practice the use of your faith daily as you serve.

Discussion Questions:

1. What is your act of reasonable service to God?
2. Is your heart that of a servant?
3. What is required of you as you serve?
4. How can you serve generously?
5. What will it require for you to truly serve others as God has called you to?

ALL-OUT PURSUIT

~

"When God pursues His children, He is on a quest to return you to a right relationship with Him. He chases after you even in your sin. God hunts for you. He willingly undertakes any challenges and will follow you into the darkest places of your life to bring deliverance to you."

Joan E. Murray, Author

9. THE PURSUIT OF THE CHOSEN

~

THE STORY OF THE prophet Hosea is amazing. If it were not written in the pages of our beloved Bible, it would be hard to believe and receive. The Lord told Hosea, the prophet, to marry a prostitute. The children of Israel had once again abandoned Him, and He was about to demonstrate to them His steadfast pursuit, unfailing love, and commitment. God is always pursuing those whom He loves and who have chosen to serve Him. In the story of Hosea, we find God willingly pursuing a people who had walked away from Him. God desires for His people to be loved and cared for and to live in abundance, not only materially but spiritually, as well. He wants you to experience wholeness and completeness in your life. This wholeness and completeness can only be found under His protection and covering.

When God pursues His children, He is on a quest to return you to a right relationship with Him. He chases after you even in your sin. God hunts for you. He willingly undertakes any challenges and will follow you into the darkest places of your life to bring deliverance to you. He does so because He does not want you to be without hope, lost, or alone. He is a God who courts His children so that He can once and for all win your affection. He pursues you to bring you back into fellowship and right relationship with Him.

The Prophet's Pursuit

Hosea the prophet was known as the prophet of restoration, and his name means "Yahweh has saved." It is therefore not surprising that God would use his life to demonstrate to you His saving and redeeming grace. The story of Hosea is a story of how God restores backsliders who have strayed away from Him. When I began to reflect on the pursuit of God, I could not help but be moved by the story of Hosea and the amazing love God has for us. Those whom God has chosen, He openly pursues with a tenderness and love that is measureless. God is consistent in His pursuit even when time and time again you turn away from Him. He faithfully and consistently pursues you, as demonstrated by the command He gave Hosea to marry the prostitute. The story of Hosea is a clear indication of the love of God for all His children. When God instructed Hosea to marry a temple prostitute, I can well imagine his reaction to God's command. It probably went something like this: "I know that I am not hearing from God. I am missing something here. What will my family and friends say about me? I will be the talk of the town because they will probably think that I have lost my mind."

God will sometimes ask you to do things that are outside of what you and others think is normal and acceptable. God told Hosea to marry this prostitute because He was about to demonstrate to the Israelites how they had once again turned their backs on Him and were worshipping idols. When Hosea obeyed God and married Gomer, God gave them children; and He used the names of the children to proclaim to the Israelites what He was about to do to them. The first child was a son, and God told them to name him Jezreel, which means, "God would now put an end to the house of Israel." The next child was a daughter and was named Lo-Ruhamah, which means, "God no longer has compassion on the Israelites." The last child was a son and was named Lo-Ammi, which means, "Israel was no longer God's people and God would no longer be their God."

God gave the Israelites a warning with the first child, and it is apparent they did not heed the warning. He told them He was removing His compassion from them, and they still proceeded in their disobedience. Finally, God decided to remove Himself from being their God, and He decided they were no longer His people. In all of this, I want you to understand that God was giving them the opportunity to show Him that they loved and would serve only Him. The heart of God must have been saddened because they still chose other gods over Him.

Today, God is still pursuing you. You might say that you are not serving idol gods because you have not created and made them with your own hands, but anything you place before God can become an idol in your life. If your health, your wealth, your family, jobs, and a host of other things cause you to worry and to exclusively focus on them; and, if they crowd God out, then those things have become idols in your life. Whatever takes your focus off God on a continual basis has become a monument or an idol in your life. God desires that you place nothing before Him. He is the first and the last, the beginning and the end of all things for you. Everything in your life should revolve around Him. If you make God the center of your life, then in whichever direction you turn, you will always be able to get a glimpse of Him because He is at the center and the core of everything you do.

Gomer

As I studied the life of Gomer, the prostitute, I could not help but wonder what devastation caused her to choose that life. In life you will go through many painful experiences; and, if you are not careful to find refuge in God, the enemy will cause you further devastation. I am sure that Gomer was wounded and needed to be rescued. God, in His infinite love, sent her a deliverer. After marrying the prophet Hosea, God lifted Gomer from a life of pain, lack, and heartache and gave her a home and family with someone well-known throughout Israel. God took her from insignificance to a life of meaning and significance. Many of you would have been content to stay there the rest of your life, but not Gomer. It is clear she had the love, protection, and covering of a husband and home, yet she walked away and went back to a life of prostitution. With her decision, it is apparent that something vital was still missing in her soul and that her old nature had not yet been crucified.

Gomer was still searching for something. I am sure in her marriage to the Prophet she encountered many challenges from the Israeli people that she had to work at overcoming. Her self-worth and self-esteem had to be at the lowest level when dealing with the challenges and new responsibilities. She must have needed constant reassurance and encouragement. Even though God had rescued and redeemed her, she did not find her full sufficiency in Him and her family. There was a void that was still in her heart. Therefore, she went back to her former life looking for what she felt was still missing but not finding it. She only found a deeper level of pain and rejection and would once again require God to rescue and reclaim her.

The Second Pursuit

Imagine with me how the prophet must have felt—his shame, embarrassment, and confusion over Gomer's desertion. He had given her his love, a home and family; but apparently, it was still not enough for her. God was not finished with Gomer or His pursuit of her. God instructed the prophet Hosea to go after her a second time and to bring her home. In obedience to God, Hosea went looking for her and found her not only back into prostitution, but she was also sold into slavery. He purchased her for fifteen pieces of silver and five bushels of barley and took her home.

God allowed Hosea to experience this desertion by his wife to show him and the Israelites how their spiritual adultery grieved Him. God was showing them how it felt each time they walked away from Him. In pursuing Gomer, God was demonstrating through the prophet the love He has for His people. He shows them that even if they turn away from Him, He will not turn away from them. He continues to pursue and pursue even when you have abandoned Him. When you sin and completely miss it, God will faithfully, tenderly, and consistently come after you. He will receive you back into the fold, even after you have broken His heart with your wrong choices.

When you return to Him, He is merciful and forgiving, never holding your sins and failures against you. He extends undeserved grace to you and never condemns you. When you return to Him, He simply says, "Welcome home, My son, My daughter, welcome home." In God's welcome, you experience His amazing forgiveness, love, and protection all over again just is if you had never left. This was the welcome Gomer received from the God who loved her deeply, even while she was in her sin. What great love the Father has for all of us that He chooses over and over to forgive us!

Discussion and Reflection

Life Application:

1. God is always pursuing you because He loves you.
2. The patience of God never runs out on you.

Challenge:

1. Daily submit to the pursuit of God.
2. Understand that you are worthy of His pursuit.

Discussion Questions:

1. Why has God chosen to pursue you?
2. What is your value?
3. How useable are you to God in your current state?
4. How do you know that God will pursue you?
5. How pleasing are you to God?

10. THE QUEST

~

GOD IS ON A quest for you! He is on the lookout for you. He is searching for you because He wants to strengthen you. The eyes of God are roaming the earth, looking for people whose hearts are set on Him. He is looking for people who desire to please Him. In His search, God is looking for people with steadfast hearts, hearts that are dedicated and committed to serving Him. When God searches and finds these people, He chooses those who are sold out to His plans and purposes for their lives. To effectively fulfill the plans of God, you must be a mature believer in whom He can establish His covenant.

If you are easily moved by every doctrine you hear, it will keep you from having a covenant relationship with God. I have known many people who have one foot in the Church and one in the world. The Bible defines them as being double-minded and easily blown away by every wind of doctrine. God wants to raise a standard for all of you who are willing to serve Him with your whole heart. The standard is to stand for Him no matter what the cost.

The above scripture is clear that when God finds these believers, He will strengthen them with His power and might, so He can fulfill great destinies through them. It is, and has always been, the desire of God to bless you, to empower you, and to give you access to everything in His Kingdom. Many of you have thus far missed out on a lot of His blessings because you have not been steadfast in your desire to please only Him. One of God's promises to you is, "He will open the windows (storehouse) of heaven and pour you out blessings that you will not have room enough to contain." (Malachi 3:10).

These storehouses have been reserved with your names on them. Because you have not pursued God fully with a desire to please Him, many of you will one day open your storehouses in Heaven and realize that there was so much more God planned for you than what you received in your earthly life. Don't let that be you. When God finds you, He fills your life with blessings, vigor, and might.

One of the blessings of being found by God is that He refreshes you with His Presence, and then He takes you to a depth and height in Him that will forever change the course of your life. He then equips you to boldly declare to the world that He is God and there is none like Him in all of heaven and earth.

God sent Hosea on a quest for Gomer because that was a demonstration of how God pursues those He loves. He does not sit back calmly and wait for your return. He is working circumstances in your life to draw you back into fellowship with Him. He goes all out searching, preparing, and readying everything that you will need when you return to Him.

Pursuing and Finding the Chosen

Here is my servant whom I have chosen, the one I love in whom I delight; I will put My Spirit on him, and he will proclaim justice to the

nations. He will not quarrel or cry out; no one will hear his voice in the streets.
A bruised reed he will not break, and a smoldering wick he will not snuff out, till he leads justice to victory. In His name nations will put their hope.

Matthew 12:18–21 (NIV)

The heart of God is tender and open toward you. He searches for His chosen people, so He can love and show His delight in them. He wants to pour the essence of Himself into you, so you can bring help to those in need. He is seeking for a people who will declare to nations His love, mercy, forgiveness, and hope. When God gets hold of these people, He demonstrates an unchanging love toward them. He begins by showing them how much they please Him and brings joy to His heart. It is a picture of parents watching and observing everything that a newborn baby does. They are aware, alert, listening, watching, and engaging in every new accomplishment. They stand and applaud with delight and joy every victory and every step.

God is a loving parent who watches your every move and cheers you on. As you grow and develop, God begins to train you to maintain peace and order around you. He teaches you how to give compassion and mercy to those who need it. He teaches you to be like Him as you dispense the same grace He has given you, to others. In every difficult circumstance, God teaches you how to gain victory and how to keep the flames of hope alive in your heart. He shows you how to hold on in the tough times. As you spend time in His Word and prayer, you will be enriched with wisdom and knowledge to overcome your struggles. When you wait on Him by spending time in His presence, He often reminds you of the many times He has already delivered you. This is for you to gain an understanding that He will deliver you again in any difficulty you face. He is truly your only deliverer.

Reasons for God's Pursuit

Before I formed you in the womb I knew you, before you were born I set you apart; I appointed you as a prophet to the nations.
Jeremiah 1:5 (NIV)

Have you ever chased after a job, relationship, or goal? In that case were you committed and willing to do whatever was necessary to attain the prize? You prayed, you fasted, and sought wise counsel to ensure that you were in proper alignment, so you would not miss the opportunity when it presented itself to you. You pursued the job, the relationship, or the goal because you knew that it would benefit your life and enrich you in many ways. God has many reasons for His pursuit of you. Before you were conceived in the minds of your parents and even before your parents came together, God had already planned your life, your days, and your destiny. Before He selected the womb in which you would be born, He formed your personality and your character. He had intimate knowledge of who you were before you were born. It is clear you existed in Him before your earthly parents even thought of you. He knew that some of you would have very direct and straightforward personalities while others would be quiet and calm.

In chapter five, I shared with you that you are created in the image of God and the Bible says that God is a Spirit. It is, therefore, clear that your spirit was with God before He gave you a body to inhabit. When God formed you, He purposely set you apart and gave you various assignments to fulfill. He made you a prophet to the nations. You are the one who will tell the truth of who He is to all those you meet. He gave you a voice so that you could testify of

His goodness to all mankind. As His prophet, you proclaim to the nations that there is no other God besides Him. By your life, examples, and words, you draw others into His Kingdom so they too can experience the fullness of life in Him.

God has called and set you over nations to expose and tear down anything that is not representative of Him. He desires that you uproot things planted in people's lives that keep them from glorifying Him. He wants to destroy anything that is given first place over Him. He overthrows any kings and kingdoms of darkness that do not represent Him. He then commissions you to plant seeds, to rebuild people, nations, and relationships, so they will be true representatives of His Kingdom.

> *"For I know the plans I have for you," declares the Lord, "plans to prosper you and not to harm you, plans to give you hope and a future. Then you will call upon Me and come and pray to Me, and I will listen to you. You will seek Me and find Me when you seek Me with all your heart. I will be found by you," declares the Lord, "and will bring you back from captivity. I will gather you from all the nations and places where I have banished you," declares the Lord, "and will bring you back to the place from which I carried you into exile."*
> *Jeremiah 29:11–14 (NIV)*

God pursues you because He has plans to bless you and give you a future filled with hope. When you seek after Him, He not only listens but also hears and moves on your behalf. God has made Himself available to your cries and your call. He is with you when you are distressed; and, when you earnestly seek after Him, you will be given an audience with Him. He is a God who is not only concerned when you are in trouble, but He is present in your joyful times because He is your life source. Once you become His, He will never fail nor abandon you. He is a very present help to you in times of trouble and will take care of your every need.

God desires to replace your mediocre plans for your life with His awesome plans for you. He said, "I know the plans I have for you, plans to bless you and not to harm you, plans to prosper you and to give you hope and a future." Can you hear His heart and feel His desire to overflow your life with good things? What He has promised to do He will do without fail. No good thing will He withhold from those who walk uprightly before Him because you belong to Him. He is in pursuit of you because He loves you, and He wants you to experience all that He designed for your life. What will you do about His pursuit?

Your Response

The "I will statements:"

- I will welcome the pursuit of God.
- I will embrace Him.
- I will return to Him with my whole heart.
- I will completely follow after Him.
- I will undertake all that He has assigned me to do.
- I will allow God to court me and shower me with His many blessings and riches.
- I will serve Him with my whole heart, soul, and mind.
- I will work hard not to disappoint Him.
- I will be found faithful in His service.
- I will not allow anything to keep me from Him.
- I will love Him with my whole being.
- I will dedicate my life to following Him.
- I will be found by Him when He pursues me.

Discussion and Reflection

Life Application:

1. God is on a quest for you.
2. God wants to live His life through you.

Challenge:

1. Plan to have an audience with God.
2. Be willing to give Him your all.

Discussion Questions:

1. What does God want from you?
2. What does God know about you?
3. How can you fulfill the plans of God for your life?
4. How will you respond to the quest of God?
5. What are you willing to do to please God?

PREPARATION IS A MUST FOR FULFILLING YOUR DESTINY

~

"Your destiny must begin with an encounter with Jesus Christ. He is the only one who can prepare you for what He has in store for you."

Joan E. Murray, Author

11. PREPARATION FOR YOUR DESTINY

~

WHEN MOST PEOPLE HEAR the word "preparation," immediately a picture comes to mind—a picture of hard work or extra time spent in training. For others, it is a feeling of readiness and anticipation of a coming event. Preparation is having the foresight of a possible outcome. It is laying the groundwork for that which you desire to take place. Still, for others, it is preparing a solid foundation on which they can build a strong and secure destiny.

In Old Testament times, we find a clear picture of the world's definition of preparation. In the book of Esther, there is a story about a woman named Vashti who was married to the king. The king held a banquet for all the people; and, on the seventh day of the banquet, He invited Vashti because he wanted to display her beauty. Vashti refused the invitation, and the king was furious. He removed her from her position and began his search for a new queen. Esther, a young Jewish girl, was chosen to marry the king; and, in due time she provided safety for the Jewish people. In

Esther's century, a woman was presented to the king only after she had spent one year being purified and prepared. For six months she was bathed in oils and myrrh to soften her skin. The next six months were spent applying all types of aromas and perfumes to her body. All bodily impurities had to be removed before she was presentable. The outer appearance had to be one of total perfection. Once the preparation process was completed, along with a host of other beautiful ladies, she was ready to be presented to the king who then made his choice. Imagine spending a year being prodded, scrubbed, perfumed, and then finally meeting the king only to learn that he did not choose you. How disappointing that must have been for many of those young ladies and how devastating for others! In your life, there is a season of preparation. This process is far different from the world's preparation process. Let us look at what is required for you to be accepted by the King of kings.

Our Acceptance

For us to be accepted by the King of Glory, our great God, the requirement is *not* one year of preparation or purification. You are acceptable just as you are when you make Jesus your personal Savior and Lord. You find instant acceptance when you acknowledge that Jesus is the Son of God by believing that He was born of a virgin, and willingly gave up His life on a horrible cross for you. When you acknowledge that He rose from the dead and is now seated at the right hand of God making intercession for you, you will find no rejection, only acceptance. To gain acceptance you must simply come to Him just as you are.

When the Holy Spirit begins to tug at your heart, you make a decision to surrender your will to Him; and He instantly comes in and begins a work of purification. Jesus our Savior is not looking for outward perfection, but He is looking for hearts that are ripe and open to Him. He is looking for those who will say, "Yes, Lord." The moment you say "Yes" to Him, He comes in, and the transformation begins. Others can see the transforming work He does on the inside of you. They can see the changes He has made in you by the way you now live. They can also recognize a change of heart.

Many years ago, the Lord told me, that if I would yield my will, my desires, and my hopes to Him; He would do a purifying work in me beginning with my heart. He also said that when people saw me, He wanted them to see a reflection of the work He had done on the inside. If you give yourself over to God, He will change you so drastically that your family and friends will be amazed at the transformation. I have met many people in recent years who shared that, when Jesus came into their lives, they were instantly delivered from all types of habits. This took place because He came in and began to wash and cleanse them from past sins. The king in the Old Testament was looking for outer beauty and perfection in the next queen. The Bible makes it clear that although men look at the outward appearance, God looks at the heart.

When God finds a heart that welcomes Him, He begins a thorough process of preparing that heart to submit and surrender to the changes He implements. God Himself takes you through the preparation stages of your journey. When you accept the beloved gift of His Son, in that instant, Jesus completely forgives you and sets you on a new course. You are presentable to God not by your outward perfection, but by an inner conviction of the heart that comes with the acceptance of His Son. In Psalms 103:12, the scripture is clear when it says, "*As far as the east is from the west so far have I removed your transgressions from you.*"

I have often wondered why God chose to say east from west and not north from south. Here is the reason. As you travel north, you will eventually arrive at the North Pole; and as you travel south, you will eventually land at the South Pole, but traveling either east or west is continuous. You keep going round and round traveling in the same direction. East from West is immeasurable! Jesus is saying that, when He forgives you and removes your sins as far as the East is from the West, His forgiveness is immeasurable! He has removed the burden and the guilt of your sins never to remember them again. He further tells you to forgive yourself and to release yourself from the penalty of your sins. He wants you to separate yourself from the sins of your past and to never look back. He wants you to be totally free in heart and mind. Free to live your life to the fullest.

Your destiny must begin with an encounter with Jesus Christ. He is the only one who can prepare you for what He has in store for you. The above scripture passage clearly states that the Word of God will teach, correct, instruct, and rebuke you as part of the preparation for training in righteousness. This preparation is to complete and prepare you for every good work. The process is necessary if you want to lay a solid foundation and build something lasting. Without a solid foundation based on solid principles and practices, you will not be equipped to overcome the obstacles you will face, as you begin to pursue your destiny. Preparation is the key to the successful attainment of your destiny.

Discussion and Reflection

Life Application:

1. In order to succeed you must prepare.
2. There is a price for everything worth having.

Challenge:

1. Do not fear the preparation process.
2. Get started right away so you can experience fulfillment.

Discussion Questions:

1. How have you been preparing for your destiny?
2. Has your preparation process been successful?
3. What has hindered you from laying a solid foundation?
4. Is your heart open to God's plans for your destiny?
5. Have you forgiven yourself for past sins/failures?

12: GOD'S PREPARATION PROCESS

~

IT GOES WITHOUT SAYING that the preparation process of
God is entirely different from ours. If you have been in a relationship with God for any length of time, you will know that during
His preparation, He often goes after things in your life that are
very deep and painful. He is after that which will cause you to
grow and develop into the likeness of Christ. Jesus makes it clear
that He is the True Vine, our life source, and we are the branches
who receive our nourishment from Him. He carefully watches
over the branches to determine which ones are bearing fruit in His
Kingdom.

In order for the branch to bear any fruit, it must stay
connected and reside within the source of life, the Vine. As the
Vine, Jesus is the stem of the plant, which gives support. He is the
only one who can direct you to your destiny and support you in
the fulfillment of it. The branch must abide with Jesus and act in
accordance with His will to get the power it needs to be effective.
Part of abiding is that you not only agree with what Jesus says but

that you also submit to His plans. You are clearly depicted, as a branch, which means you are a part of the stem of the plant and not the plant itself. A branch is an offshoot of the stem of the tree. Apart from the vine, a branch will wither and die. As the branch, you must be intentional in your desire to stay connected to the Vine. This connection is not automatic. It must be planned into your schedule and nourished daily with time spent in the Word, prayer, and communication with God.

The Cleansing

Have you ever been at a place in your life when all seems well? For a change, everything was going along peacefully. You found contentment and were happy to finally get there after much struggle. For a season, you continued to enjoy this contentment, then one day something happened that knocked you sideways, and you were plunged into a season of pain, hardship, and in some cases devastation. The Bible is clear that the devil is like a roaring lion seeking whom he may devour (1 Peter 5:8). It did not say he was a roaring lion but that he *is like* a roaring lion. I have seen pictures of lions without teeth and that is the picture of what the devil looks like. He seems tough and scary, but when he opens his mouth to roar at you, you realize to your amazement that he is toothless. When you are plunged into seasons of pain and hurt, the toothless devil is roaring; and his roar can cause you some pain, as well as concern. God knows that the devil will roar into your life from time to time. His roar can be painful, but God will use the pain to begin His cleansing work in you. He begins to prune away things that seem perfectly fine and necessary to you.

I remember a time when I was finally in a season when I thought I was going to get some rest from my struggles and valleys. In the midst of this season, a friend decided to share some of my personal struggles with some of her friends. This friend had known me for a long time, and she knew I was a private person, yet she chose to share my personal information. This caused me great pain, and in the midst of my pain, I asked God why. His response was, "I am in the process of pruning unnecessary relationships out of your life so I can draw you closer to Me." I can truly say the pruning was as painful as it was necessary. I learned to talk to God more and to depend on Him more than I did friends. Through this pruning season, I began a journey of developing a closer relationship with Christ.

When God begins the cleansing process in your life, the Holy Spirit comes in and begins to teach you how to control your sinful nature and desires. In 1 Peter, the Apostle Peter beseeches you to live free from sin. To beseech means to come alongside or near to someone as close as you can get. Then plead with the person to take some course of action against sin in his or her life. The Holy Spirit does the beseeching in you. He is constantly showing you areas that you need to let go of and turn over to God. To beseech is an urgent call for a change in lifestyle. It is a flashing light used to get your attention. The Holy Spirit in His gentle way nudges you in your heart, when you are outside the will of God, and urges you to return to His protection. As a believer, you must have a disciplined, rigid, and committed mindset to combat the attack of the enemy in your life. You must remember that you are a stranger and pilgrim in this world, and you are on a journey to your destination, which is Heaven. You want this journey to be a powerful one of victory, so you must be on guard against the enemy's attempts to distract, disappoint, and destroy you along the way.

The plan of God for you is to live your life separate from the world. He desires that you deliberately withdraw yourself from things that would destroy you and for you to put distance between yourself and temptation. The Bible clearly instructs you to flee temptation. You are not supposed to reason out whether you are strong enough to overcome it but to flee when it is presented to you. As a believer, you must be intentional in your fight against sin and put distance between you and sin. You should always remember that your flesh is never content until it is in control and ruling over you. You must guard your heart because what goes in will eventually come out. Your struggles will bring to the surface what is buried in your heart. The condition of your heart will affect all that you do because whatever is in your heart is what you will speak over your life. Your destiny is impacted by what is in your heart. You will become what you think about and meditate on regularly.

If you do not consistently guard your heart against the impact of the enemy's lies, and his attempts to deceive and get you off course, you will end up living in mediocrity, never attaining the great things God has planned for you. God's process of preparation is to ensure that you are whole and complete, lacking nothing. Therefore, He will weed out, pull up, and prune anything in you that will keep you from growing and producing fruit in His Kingdom. Though the process can be painful at times, it is well worth it, if you truly desire to become transformed into His likeness.

Discussion and Reflection

Life Application:

1. The preparation of God is deep and meaningful.
2. The preparation of God is ongoing.

Challenge:

1. Allow God to do a deep work in your heart.
2. Submit to the pain of preparation because it will eventually get you to your destiny.

Discussion Questions:

1. How connected are you to Christ?
2. Are you afraid to let God do a deep cleansing work in you?
3. Have you experienced the pain of preparation?
4. Do you flee from sin?
5. How good are you at guarding your heart?

13: SUBMISSION TO THE PROCESS

~

YOU SERVE AN OMNISCIENT GOD who promised you eternal life from before time began (Titus 1:2). God knew that Adam would fail and implemented His plan for your redemption before the foundation of the world. I like to think that God the Father, God the Son, and God the Holy Spirit had a meeting in Heaven to determine which of them would redeem mankind. One of them had to decide to be the perfect substitute for us. He had to yield up His title, be willing to be born as a baby and suffer the hurt and pain of rejection in order to bring us eternal life.

The decision that Jesus made to be our Savior required the submission of His position, authority, and will to that of the Father. It took love and a willingness to die for others. In His submission, He accepted unjust punishment. When He was wrongfully accused, He did not in turn accuse others; and when He was threatened, He did not respond in kind. He submitted to the preparation process because He understood what was at stake. We are told, "Who for the joy that was set before Him, endured the cross, despising the shame, and has sat down at the right hand of the throne of God" (Heb. 12:2). He willingly gave up His throne, splendor, worship, and adoration to save a people who would mock, ridicule, scorn, and then hang Him on the cross. He submitted willingly, fully understanding what He would face. Jesus is our perfect example of submission —though right, He gave up His rights and went to the cross to redeem us. He submitted in love and by love.

Our Submission

For you to totally submit, you must model yourself after the example of Jesus. You must acknowledge that submission is a part of the will of God for your life. You must first yield your will over to God with the full understanding that He will mold and shape you into the image and likeness of His Son. As you begin submitting to the preparation process, the Bible encourages you to submit to one another; to earthly authority, to men, to leaders, and to masters. To willingly submit yourself to these authorities, you should know that there is no loss of dignity, but there will be an increase in the power of God in your life. Submission is not a subservient word or position.

It takes a powerful person to truly submit to another's authority. Submission requires obedience even when you are not in full agreement. It is the total surrender of what you may think and believe to allow someone else the opportunity to be right. That takes power! Have you ever been in a heated discussion and knew without a doubt that you were right; but, in order to bring peace to the situation, you backed off? That is submission. Even though you were right, you yielded to another person's desire to be right to bring harmony. You gave up your right to be right, and that decision has the power to transform your relationships and change the lives of the people who receive the benefits of your submission.

The Transformation

Many years ago, while on a new job, I was at a meeting in Chicago when I experienced what submission required. Part of my job responsibility was to plan meetings and events. During one of these meetings, I had an intense discussion with my supervisor over an item that I had ordered for the meeting. She insisted that I ordered the wrong item; and when I attempted to tell her that I had consulted with the service manager at the hotel, who assured me that the item was correct, this just irritated her further. My supervisor did not believe me and chose to make a big deal out of the situation. I attempted several times to bring clarification and finally gave up in frustration. I told her to contact them herself, which she did.

She called them and they took the time to clarify it with her. I had eventually yielded my will and submitted to her even though I knew I was right. I yielded because the discussion was getting heated and producing no results. After the service manager explained the situation, I tried to remain humble and let the issue pass, but I later discovered that it had generated some resentment in my supervisor. Though I submitted, I still had to deal with the aftereffects of that discussion. I realized later that had I submitted to her sooner, it would have produced better results. It takes power to submit when you know you are right, but submit to keep the peace and to ensure that relationships are not damaged beyond repair.

Jesus understood that when He submitted to the cross it would eventually produce a great harvest. As you submit, you must understand that though you may not see immediate results, God will indeed vindicate you. Submission can transform a life because you allow someone else the opportunity to be right. The transformation will come when they, in humility, acknowledge the great sacrifice you made and allow God to correct them when they are wrong. When the person acknowledges that they are wrong, repents, and asks your forgiveness, that act of humility can transform your relationship and build a foundation of mutual trust and respect. You are in a position of power when you learn to submit because God will never let you fail as you willingly give way to someone else. The moment that you allow another person the opportunity to be right, you demonstrate to God that you are just like His Son who willingly gave His all for you.

The Cost of Submission

Study to show yourselves approved unto God, a workman that needeth not to be ashamed, rightly dividing the word of truth.
II Timothy 2:15 (KJV)

To be successful in life you will often pay a price for your success. The preparation that is required for your success can come with a heavy price tag. This is not to scare you but to let you know that you must determine in your heart that you are prepared to go all the way with God so you can succeed. You must determine that there is nothing too difficult that will prevent you from persevering until you attain your destiny. As I think back over the four years I spent in college, I can truly say that it was a great expense for me. Since I was responsible for the entire bill, I had to work, so I found a job in a retail store. I went to school from seven in the morning to twelve noon on Mondays through Thursdays. I then worked from one in the afternoon to nine in the evenings. When I arrived home from work, I studied and prepared for the next day. During those four years, I slept only five hours a night.

Many of you can tell the same story. There was a cost, a sacrifice, to attain the things that you have thus far accomplished with your life. You willingly paid the price because you had a goal in mind. There is a cost to prepare yourself for what God has in store for you. Preparation is required so that you can be effective in your assignments. There are various ways to prepare, as we will further discover in this chapter.

Time Commitment

Your destiny requires time to plan and to prepare. In your time commitment, you should have seasons when you cannot be reached by phone. Often the phone keeps you distracted when you should be focusing on the task before you. I cannot begin to tell you how often the phone would ring the moment I sat down to spend time with God or to begin working on a project that would lead to my destiny. I finally learned that ignoring it was not the key because the ringing would still disturb me. So, I began turning it off during times of study and preparation so my mind and my heart could become focused on what was before me. You must decide how you will commit your time. Will you spend hours on the phone or in front of the television, when you have projects that need your attention? The television is a distraction for many of you. You can spend hours of unproductive time watching it and living out other people's dreams instead of pursuing your own dreams. You must develop a schedule and a plan of action about how you will use your time. Remember, each day God has given you enough grace and time to accomplish what He has for you to do. If you use this time wisely, you will not miss a step in the preparation process.

Time Alone

Each of you must have time alone to think and process the things that God is speaking to your spirit. This is time spent in the presence of God to ascertain what He has for you to do, and to obtain a plan of action from Him. In your "alone" time you will pray, read the Word, and wait in the presence of God listening for His instructions. Each time you get before the Lord and petition Him, He will answer you. You often miss hearing His answers because you do not wait long enough in His presence for Him to speak. You can become impatient if He does not speak in the first two minutes and walk away without an answer from Him. I have been guilty of this and then wondered why God has not spoken to me. It is not that He has not spoken. It is that you are too busy to be still and hear His voice.

The Bible tells you that the Holy Spirit speaks in a still, small voice. He will not yell over the ringing of the phone, the noise of the television, or even the roar of normal conversations. I have not experienced many times in my life when the Holy Spirit has yelled or shouted to get my attention. The few times He has done so were to give me a warning of impending danger. When God speaks to your heart, you need time to ponder and reflect on what you have heard and to wait for further instructions. A key to your success as you spend time alone with God is to know that His anointing is on the instructions that you hear, receive, and obey.

Study Time

Second Timothy tells you to study to show yourself approved unto God. You study to develop an intimate relationship with God. You study to know Him and to understand His will and His ways. You study so you can be an imitator of Him and live the life He has destined for you. As you study, you gain knowledge and are able to share that knowledge with others. When you know what God would do in any situation, you are able to pattern yourself after Him and give hope to others. It has been said that people do not often listen to what is being said, but they watch what you do and model that.

In your preparation season, you must study to demonstrate to others what God is revealing to you. When you fill your heart with the Word of God, and fill your mind with thoughts of Him, you can effectively share what you have learned with those He puts in your path. You do not study to boast about what you know, but to get to know God in all His glory. You carve out time to study because you want to spend time with God and give Him pleasure. It is pleasing to God when you daily set time aside to spend with Him. He has given you His Word so that you can study to know His will and plan for your destiny. Each time you open the pages of His Word, you encounter Him in a new and fresh way. The Bible is alive and powerful, and every word was designed to bring hope and healing to the believer. As you read and apply the principles that are contained in the Word of God, you are guaranteed a life of blessings, fullness, and prosperity.

The Sacrifice

The preparation season of your life will also require a sacrifice. The things you would readily do may have to be rescheduled. You will miss out on some fun activities because God is drawing you into His Presence for further instructions. You will sometimes have to sacrifice relationships. Some of your current friendships will not have the right ingredients to last in the next level of your destiny. You will have to leave some relationships behind because not everyone will understand your sacrifice, as you prepare. Some people will tell you that it does not require "*all that*" to do what God has called you to do. They will not understand your dedication to the process or your willingness to give your time to it.

Others will not be able to understand, agree, or even comprehend your destiny and the plans you have to attain it. In the back of their minds, there will always be the thought that they knew you "back then." Since they have witnessed many of your mistakes and failures, they will not believe that God is speaking to you about the great destiny He has in store for you. If you are not careful and do not have a willingness to let go of these relationships, you can become discouraged from pursuing God and His plans for you. It truly requires a sacrifice to go all the way with God. It is called a living sacrifice.

Living Sacrifice

You can no longer gratify your flesh with what you say and do. You must subject your flesh to the guidance of the Holy Spirit who lives in you. Your spirit was created to have control over your entire life. The flesh was not designed to rule you, but because of sin many of us are controlled by our fleshly desires. In the preparation process, you learn how to subject your flesh to your spirit by doing what is necessary and required. Preparation causes you to suppress what you would normally do, so you can accomplish what is set before you. Each time you say "No" to the flesh and its desires, you are saying "Yes" to God and His will for you. As you sacrifice time on the phone, watching the television, and letting go of some unhealthy relationships so you can draw nearer to God, He will draw near to you and fill you with more of Himself. There is a sacrifice for anything that is worth attaining and it requires dying to self. Make it your prayer that the Lord will teach you how to crucify your flesh, so your spirit can rule and govern every single decision that you make.

Discussion and Reflection

Life Application:

1. Submission is a requirement for your success.
2. There is a cost to attaining your destiny.

Challenge:

1. Do not fear submitting to others because God is watching out for you.
2. Allow God to humble you as you submit to Him.

Discussion Questions:

1. What keeps you from submitting to others?
2. Does the thought of submission scare you?
3. What keeps you from spending time alone with God?
4. What do you enjoy most about studying the Word of God?
5. What are you willing to sacrifice to go all the way with God?

14: THE NEED FOR PREPARATION

∾

DURING THE EARLY YEARS of my life, my grandmother, Elizabeth, taught me about the need for preparation. She not only taught me how to prepare for life, but she also taught me what was needed and necessary in the preparation process. The first thing she revealed to me that required preparation was my need for a Savior in the form of Jesus Christ. From an early age, she took me to church but did not push me to accept Christ. She regularly prayed and prepared the way for me to encounter Him.

When I gave my heart to the Lord, at the age of twelve, she was the first to share it with the family. I must say that many of my family members told me I was too young, and it would not stick. I am here to tell you that I was not too young, and I have been saved for many years because my grandmother prepared me to encounter my Savior. Each of you must prepare those you love to encounter the Savior no matter how young they are. God begins to work in the hearts of His children from an early age, so they will not miss any time in their relationship with Him. Each night my grandmother helped me prepare my attire for the next school day, and each morning she prepared breakfast and lunch for me. In all of this, my grandmother recognized and fulfilled a need in me. She equipped me with what I needed to ensure that I produced good work. You were born with a need to prepare for life, your future, and your destiny. This need to prepare is inherent in your nature. It is a need that was given to you by a loving God to mature you during each phase of your life.

Preparation fully equips you to live life to its fullest. When you plan and take the time to prepare, you are fully supplied with all that you need to accomplish whatever task is placed before you. God desires that you are thoroughly equipped for every good work. He wants you to be fully decked out and no longer ill-equipped to handle the storms that you will encounter in life. When you understand this need to be prepared, you will be able to go anywhere and do anything because you will be prepared for any event. I have flown frequently over the past ten years; and, as I prepare for each trip, part of my preparation is to pray for protection in the air. I pray that the angels of the Lord encamp about us as we fly, and I pray for the pilots and the crew. Many times, I arrive at the departure gate to observe the pilots walking around the aircraft and below it, checking that all is well. The pilots are in the preparation process before departure. There is a need to ensure the aircraft is in good working condition and ready to safely transport the passengers to their destination. None of you is aware of what lies ahead of you; but, as you prepare, you are equipping yourself to handle the storms of life.

Your greatest preparation is done through time spent studying the Word of God. As you study and meditate on the Word, God speaks to your heart and brings comfort and assurance. You also prepare when you spend time in prayer, seeking God for His direction and protection. There is a great need to renew your mind daily because if you neglect to do so, many of you will not make it across the ocean of life or through the storms you will encounter. Whatever you have planned for your life, make sure that you understand the need for preparation, which will ensure your success.

Reasons for Preparation

The Lord's servant must not quarrel; instead, he must be kind to everyone, able to teach, not resentful. Those who oppose him, he must gently instruct, in the hope that God will grant them repentance leading them to a knowledge of the truth.
II Timothy 2:24–25 (NIV)

Here Paul clearly states to Timothy what it means to serve the Lord. You serve the Lord when you serve others. In His service, you prepare yourself to be kind, gentle, and teachable as He instructs you to lead His people. If you are unprepared, you will fail when you encounter people who try your patience and are unwilling to be taught.

The preparation process enables you to stand when you face trials. It is clear in the above passage of scripture that time spent with God in preparation will empower you to take care of the needs of others. In God's preparation, you learn to put away the desire to be quarrelsome when you are not getting your way. In your daily service to God, you will encounter people whom you might feel are not reachable and are unapproachable. In these encounters, you must have gentleness, as you instruct them in the things of God. You must ask for God's help and guidance so you can direct the people to Him. As you direct them to God and they come to a place of repentance, God will reveal His love and truth to them.

The enemy often uses resentment to keep you from being helpful to others. People will do and say things to you that are hurtful and are not a true representation neither of who you are or of your abilities. As a result, you can develop feelings of resentment toward them. Resentment causes you not to hear clearly and not to practice forgiveness quickly. When you are resentful, you do not give people the benefit of the doubt. Have you found when you have taken on resentment that you rehearse the injustice over and over in your mind? The more you rehearse it the more resentful you become, which keeps you from forgiving and receiving the forgiveness you need from the Lord. When this happens, you easily abandon people when they need your help the most because your view is clouded with offense.

The Bible instructs you to let go of resentment because it is a poison that the devil releases to keep you trapped and unproductive. Preparation time spent with God gives you the inner strength and assurance you need when you have to face difficulties. As you serve God by serving others, God will remind you that, when the going gets tough, He is always with you and will never fail you. When you spend time with God and are prepared to be used by Him, He will give you a supernatural infilling of His divine power, which will supercharge you when you need it the most. All of you have the same need to prepare, so you are fully equipped and ready to encounter the risen Lord at His second coming.

Our Preparation Process

There is a permissive will of God and a perfect will of God. Many Christians live in the permissive will of God but not in His perfect will for their lives. In His permissive will, God will allow you certain things you ask for even though it may not be in His best plan for your life. In this permissive will, you are given permission to make some of your own choices. Often you obtain permission because you have nagged, begged, and pleaded with God so often that He simply turns you over to do as you will. Many of you make your choices in disobedience to what He has told you to do. He allows you the choice to use your own will and intellect to make your decision. He does so because He knows that each decision and each choice will provide a lesson in your life, often a painful lesson, which will help you in your growth and development.

Consider the story of Adam and Eve. God permitted them to eat of every tree in the garden except one, but they disobeyed Him and ate from the very tree He told them not to. God was neither asleep nor unaware when they made their choice. He knew exactly where they were and what they were about to do, and He could have stopped them at any time by overriding their will. Since He created them with a free will, this gave them the ability to choose, and they chose to disobey Him. This was not the perfect plan of God for them or the human race, but He had to abide by their decision.

In His permissive will, He allowed them to make their own choice. He does the same thing with you and me. Some of you clearly heard God when He told you not to marry the individual you did; not to take that particular job or move to a certain location, but you chose to ignore Him. Therefore, in His permissive will, He allows you to make the decision you are set on making. By your decisions, you have learned some painful lessons in life, which He will use to bring Him glory. Each decision you make comes with a lesson, and each lesson can benefit you if you turn it over to God and allow Him to use these lessons to be a blessing to others. God will not waste a single difficulty, trial, or devastation that you have gone through. He will use the good, the bad, and the evil things that have happened to you and will work all things together for your good because He loves you and has called you to fulfill a great purpose in Him (Romans 8:28).

The Perfect Will of God

In the perfect will of God, you receive His instructions. Unlike Adam and Eve, you choose to do things His way. You do not disobey Him but obey His commands. You learn to listen, hear, and obey the instructions of the Holy Spirit when He speaks to your heart. When you hear Him, you submit your will over to Him and do what He tells you to do. You accept that God is in full control, and you give way to whatever He wants to do. In His perfect will for you, it is no longer you that lives, but Christ living through you (Gal. 2:20). In His will you listen by engaging your mind, heart, ears, eyes, and your entire being on what God is saying and doing. When you hear Him, you do exactly what you are told by following His instructions. You then obey what you hear by actively engaging yourself with God and allowing Him to become fully engaged with you, in you, and through you. To obey Him means that you follow His plan, do what He tells you to, and come to an understanding that He knows what is best for you. You blindly follow where He leads because you know He will never lead you down the wrong path for your life nor will He ever fail you.

In the preparation process, you will also learn it is and always has been the plan of God to increase you and take you from glory to glory in Him. Therefore, choose to make God a daily part of your agenda by scheduling time to meet with Him face-to-face. As you go through the process of conforming to His perfect will, you must get organized so you can have clear insight into where God is taking you. As you humbly submit to His will and His way, He will lead you down the best path for your life. Choose today to live in the perfect will of God and not in His permissive will and prepare yourself to receive His abundant blessings. The preparation process is the key to knowing and living out the perfect will of God for your life and for fulfilling your great destiny.

Discussion and Reflection

Life Application:

1. You need to prepare so you can fulfill your destiny.
2. There is a preparation process for each person.

Challenge:

1. Daily spend time preparing by praying, reading, and meditating on the Word of God.
2. Choose the perfect will of God and not His permissive will.

Discussion Questions:

1. Why is preparation so necessary?
2. What are the results of preparation?
3. What will it personally cost you to prepare?
4. How can preparation ensure your success?
5. Are you living in the permissive or perfect will of God for your life?

WALKING IN THE FULLNESS OF YOUR DESTINY

~

"Every great destiny comes with testing, and Abraham failed a number of his tests. If Abraham could fail and still fulfill such a great destiny, you and I have tremendous hope that God will use us to fulfill our destinies even though we have failed Him at times."

Joan E. Murray, Author

15: FULFILLING YOUR DESTINY

~

ALL OF YOU AT one time or another have felt an urgency to accomplish something with your life. Coupled with these feelings is a desire to know why you were born and why you are here. Throughout this book, I have given you some signs to look for in the process of discovering your destiny. Now, let us embark on the journey to discover how you can fulfill your destiny. Fulfillment comes in many different forms. Some of you are fulfilled with a good-paying job, a good family life, money in the bank, and a nice home; but then there are others who have a desire for more. It is important to know that God has designed each of you differently and each one must discover what will bring ultimate fulfillment. In your search to discover what fulfills you, do not compare your satisfaction level with another person's.

To be fulfilled is to be satisfied with what you have and where you are in your life. It is a feeling of contentment when you have realized or fulfilled a dream or a goal. This feeling of gratification comes when you learn to rest in the promises of God to take what

He says about you to heart and then begin to apply it to your own life. The fulfillment you experience in your life, and in your walk with Him ensures that you are prepared and equipped not only to discover but to fulfill your destiny.

To those who are wondering, *"What is my destiny?"* The answer is the perfect plan of God for your life and that which you were born to do. Your destiny is the reason you exist, and it is your destination in life. God has predestined you to live a life that will not only bring you joy and peace but will also bring you fulfillment and completion. His destiny for you is beyond what you can think, ask, or imagine. For those of you who have a great imagination— take your greatest dream, multiply it by a thousand, and understand that God plans to go exceedingly abundantly above that. His destiny for you will take Him, you, and others to fulfill. God will take you on a journey of a lifetime to fulfill your destiny if you will open your heart to receive what He is saying to you. God took Abraham and Joseph on an adventurous journey in the process of fulfilling their destinies.

Abraham's Journey to His Destiny

In Chapter 1, we discovered that Abraham was willing to obey and follow God in the fulfillment of his destiny. When he left his homeland and began walking toward his destiny, he chose separation from all that was familiar to him. He believed a voice, which he could not see, to be the voice of the true and living God. He then put action to his belief and began pursuing God for further instructions and directions. As an acknowledgment that he heard and that he would obey the instructions, Abraham built an altar where God spoke to him. He memorialized the place by setting up a monument. This monument was a reminder to him about when and where God spoke, and that God would be faithful to do what He said. Abraham traveled throughout the land looking for the right place to begin his purpose. He ended up in Egypt because there was a famine in the land of Canaan. He did not yet fully understand that God was His source and that God could provide for him even in the midst of famine. God allowed Abraham to journey to Egypt because it would become the place of testing and preparation for his destiny. Every great destiny comes with testing, and Abraham failed a number of his tests. If Abraham could fail and still fulfill such a great destiny, you and I have tremendous hope that God will use us to fulfill our destinies even though we have failed Him at times.

Abraham's first test was a *trust test.* Would he trust God amid famine and in an unknown territory with his life and the life of his wife? Would he also trust God to provide for their needs in the midst of famine? His second test was an *integrity test.* Would he trust God to protect him from the attacks of the enemy? He failed both tests because he went to Egypt for provision during the famine and he lied to the king of Egypt, saying Sarah was his sister instead of his wife. He did this because she was very beautiful and he feared that he would be killed for her. As a result, the king took her into his palace and made her a part of his harem. God, through a dream, sent a warning to the king that Sarah was Abraham's wife, and to return her to him unharmed or he would suffer severe consequences. The king obeyed God and returned Abraham's wife to him, so they left Egypt and returned to Canaan, their prepared place.

God blessed Abraham by giving him livestock, silver, and gold and made him wealthy beyond his wildest dreams, but he still had not produced the promised heir. Abraham went through yet another test, this time it was a *faithfulness test.* Following the advice of his impatient wife Sarah, he produced a son by Sarah's servant, Hagar. Abraham was unfaithful to God because God had already promised that his heir would come through Sarah and not the servant girl. He knew the promise yet proceeded in his disobedience. Even when Abraham disobeyed God, God did not forget him or the promises He had made to him. At one hundred years old, he and Sarah finally produced the promised heir, his son. Isaac. On his journey to his destiny, Abraham waited twenty-five years to see the manifestation of the promise. Because he waited and continued to believe and trust God, he received a great reward. With the birth of the promised son, Abraham began the fulfillment of his destiny on this journey of a lifetime.

Joseph's Journey to His Destiny

In Chapter 2, we discover that Joseph's brothers sold him into slavery, and he ended up in Egypt in Potiphar's house. Joseph found himself alone and in a strange country with no one to depend on but God for support, encouragement, and direction because of his isolation. Joseph was at a place in his life where he had to depend and rely totally on God. This season in his life would develop a deeper and more abiding relationship with God. God would become his refuge, his confidant, and the only one who would hear his cry and grant him deliverance. In his journey, Joseph encountered times of testing that would equip him for the destiny God had selected him to fulfill.

His first test came in the form of Potiphar's wife who tried to seduce him while he was a servant in his master's house. This first test was a *flesh test*. In this test, God allowed Joseph to be tempted so that he could see what was in his heart. When he faced this test, he told Potiphar's wife that he would not sin against his God. I want you to notice that Joseph's focus was on God, and he was determined to do nothing that would be a stain on God's name. His next test was a *position test*. In this test, Joseph found himself in prison serving thirteen years for a crime he did not commit. The prison was a place of hardship and lack for a young man who was beloved and favored at home. Joseph, in this lowly position, continued to trust God and to serve Him with all his heart. He did not have an attitude because he was demoted but served where he was planted.

He then faced a *heart test*. Would he be bitter and unforgiving toward God for allowing him to be in this situation? Would bitterness take root in his heart toward his brothers who sold him into slavery? He chose to allow God to process and prepare him through this time of hardship. While he oversaw Potiphar's house, he encountered the *integrity test*. He handled Potiphar's possessions as if they were his own. He did not take anything that was not given to him, and he served Potiphar with integrity because ultimately, he was serving God. Joseph also went through a *relationship test*. Would his relationship with God suffer because of what he was going through, and would he blame God for where he was? When many believers are facing hardships, they will either turn away from God or turn to others for help, and some will even walk away from a relationship with God.

Joseph did not turn away from God nor did he look to others for help. Even though he understood that God could have prevented all that he was going through, he trusted that God had a greater plan that he could not yet see. In his final test, the *trust test,* Joseph modeled for us an example of a man who was totally sold out to God and served Him with consistency even in the darkest moments of his life. He remained faithful through all these tests and God was with him along this journey. He was an encourager in prison and used his gift of dream interpretation to help and bless others.

Joseph was thrown into prison for being a dreamer and for sharing his dreams with those who could not receive them. Those very dreams catapulted him to greatness in Egypt. God blessed him beyond anything he could think, dream, or imagine, and he became the second most prominent and wealthy man in all of Egypt and the surrounding areas. God restored his family and used his gift to save nations from starvation including his father and brothers. It took commitment to God, dedication to His plans, extreme trust, and unwavering faith for Joseph to reach his destiny. The question is worth asking, "What will it take for you to accomplish your destiny?"

Journey to Your Destiny

I am going to send an Angel before you to protect you on the way and bring you to the place I have prepared.
Exodus 23:20 (CSB)

It is exciting and encouraging to know that God does not expect you to discover your destiny on your own. He has put a plan in place to get you to your place of destiny. In His Kingdom, angels are assigned to do what God bids them to. In the above passage of scripture, God makes it clear that He will send angels before you to protect and bring you safely to the place He has prepared for you. As believers, angels have been assigned to us, the heirs of salvation. They are assigned to guard, protect, help, and watch over us to ensure that we do not come to harm. As you begin the journey to your destination, keep in mind that God has already prepared the place that He has for you. He has gone before you to annihilate any enemies that would hinder you from taking rightful occupancy of your promised land.

Just recall the story of the children of Israel's journey out of captivity. As God delivered them from Egyptian bondage and sent them on a journey to their promised land, a place flowing with milk and honey, He sent terror and confusion ahead of them to route the inhabitants of the land that they were to occupy. Each enemy of God and His chosen people were displaced, destroyed, dispatched, or given a clear understanding that God would defend and deliver His people even to the death of other nations. God goes before you and drives out the inhabitants little by little so that your land will not be desolate or overrun with evil when you get there. On your journey, He is also preparing you to accept and receive what He has in mind for you to do. Each step of the journey is a step in the preparation process. When your steps are paved with difficulties, God is building stamina in you. He wants you to be strong and courageous, ready to take up occupancy in your land no matter what obstacles you may face. It is important in the journey that you do not give way to complaining, disobedience, or frustration. These things will keep you from getting to your destination.

On their journey, the Israelites were disobedient and complained so much that God was fed up with them. Those who were twenty years and older died in the wilderness and did not make it into the Promised Land to enjoy the blessings that were reserved for them. Remember, the devil is real, and it is His job to keep you from fully discovering and enjoying what God has in store for you, so he will keep you in a cycle of murmuring and complaining. Be on guard and watch, as well as pray, so you will not be foiled by his attempt to keep you from your destination.

Like Abraham, you must build an altar and set up a monument at the place where God spoke to you about his plans for your life. In our modern times, you may not be able to set up a physical altar, but you can do so by documenting when God spoke and what He said. If you are not one to journal, you may want to start doing so. In journaling, you can document the day, date, and time God spoke to you. When God brings about His promises in your life, you can go back to your journal and document the date He fulfilled His promises to you. It is important that all of you have *markers* in your lives. Markers are events that remind you of the faithfulness of God to deliver you through difficult times. They also remind you of the many times He has blessed and moved in the situations of your life. These markers are your monuments to remind you that, if He did it for you once, He will be faithful to do it again whenever you are in need. These markers are your hope line. They are there when you feel boxed in and hopeless and cannot see your way clearly.

When you feel hemmed in and without hope, God will spark in your memory the times He delivered you and will remind you that He is there and He is a very present help in trouble. God will use these markers in your life as reminders to you not to lose hope, faith, or confidence in Him. Without your hope in God, and reliance on Him, you will go under and not over when you face life's difficulties. On your journey to your destination, begin to document the many blessings that you discovered along the way. Memorialize the place God spoke to you and what He said. When you face difficult transitions, remind yourself that He is a faithful God, and His mercies are new to you each day. Remember His unfailing love for those He has called and chosen to fulfill great destinies in Him. He will never forsake nor abandon you. You have His promise, so enjoy this great adventure and this journey of a lifetime.

Discussion and Reflection

Life Application:

1. Life is filled with adventure.
2. Your life begins with a journey.

Challenge:

1. Go on an adventure with God.
2. Memorialize the place God spoke to you.

Discussion Questions:

1. Have you ever been on an adventure with God?
2. Where did the adventure lead you?
3. What is keeping you from experiencing the fullness of God?
4. How are you doing on your journey to your destiny?
5. Are you failing your times of testing?

16: HINDRANCES TO FULFILLING YOUR DESTINY

~

YOU HAVE ALL ENCOUNTERED times when you have been hindered from getting something you truly wanted. On the journey to your destiny, many of you will encounter hindrances that are designed to discourage you from the pursuit. You must recognize these hindrances and allow God to show you how to overcome them. It is the enemy's job to discourage and keep you from moving forward, but it is your job to resist him and overcome all of the hindrances he places in your path on the way to your destiny. He is on an outright attack to keep the blessings of God from flowing into your life.

When he tries his best to hinder you, remember that the greater One lives in you, and He gives you the power to overcome every situation. You must tap into the power source, which is the Holy Spirit so that you can withstand any attempts of the enemy to keep you in mediocrity and away from your destination.

Doubt

"Have faith in God," Jesus answered. "I tell you the truth, if anyone says to this mountain, 'Go, throw yourself into the sea,' and does not doubt in his heart but believes that what he says will happen, it will be done for him. Therefore I tell you, whatever you ask for in prayer, believe that you have received it and it will be yours."
Mark 11:22–24 (NIV)

One of the greatest tools of the enemy to keep you from the destiny that God has reserved for you is doubt. Doubt keeps you from hearing clearly and from moving in any direction. Doubt can be crippling to the degree that you are afraid to move toward your goals. When you doubt, you are unable to hear instructions from God clearly and can develop a lack of confidence in His ability to help you. In your doubt, you do not expect anything good to happen to you. You often expect the worst in the situations of your life. Doubt is a heart condition. It keeps you from believing that anything is possible. If you cannot see or understand that all things are possible to those who believe God, then you are unable to dream and to accomplish those dreams.

Doubt causes your view to be cloudy and you cannot get a clear picture of what you need. When you are in doubt, you are unsure of yourself and not able to make the right decisions or any decision at all. In your doubting, you often wonder if God cares about you and whether He will answer when you call to Him. Your doubting blocks your communion with God. It clogs the communication channel between Him and you. In Mark 11, God tells you that if you do not harbor doubt in your heart, you can speak to the mountains in your life, and they must obey you. When you walk out of doubt and into faith, whatever you ask and believe God for, will be yours. Shake off the spirit of doubt, put on the clothing of faith, and begin to move toward the fulfillment of your destiny.

Unbelief

Have you ever experienced times when you wondered if God was really there and whether He heard as you prayed to Him? While teaching a recent Bible study, I asked the attendees what was keeping them from a consistent prayer life. The response from most of them was that they were unsure as to whether God was hearing them. Because of their unbelief, they could not commit to consistency in prayer. This lack of consistency was keeping them from getting to the best plan of God for their lives. Unbelief can be damaging to your relationship with God because you think that many of the things, He desires to give you are too far-fetched and unbelievable. As you battle unbelief, you can be skeptical in your outlook on life and doubt what you may be able to accomplish. Your unbelief will keep you from obtaining anything of great value. God designed you with the ability to believe and trust Him.

From an early age, most of you learn to trust your parents, have confidence in what they say, and in their ability to provide and take care of you. God is your Father, and He desires that you have the same level of belief and trust in His ability to hear and provide for you. When you lack belief, you are literally saying to God, "You are not big enough or great enough to handle the things that are a problem for me."

Consider this, when you raised your hand and stood up to accept Jesus as your personal Savior and Lord, you did so by believing that He was born of the Virgin Mary and was the Son of God. You also believed that He died and rose from the grave, and as a result, you now have eternal life. If you truly believe that and have given your life over to Him, you must use the same level of belief, trust, faith, and confidence to know that God wants to bless you abundantly. You must also come to know that He will withhold no good thing from you because you are His beloved child. Unbelief in God is not the proper position for any of His children.

Without your belief in Him, you will not be able to accomplish anything with your life. The devil knows that God is real because he lived with Him before he was kicked out of heaven. He understands if you ever get a revelation of how true and real God is and that He is absolutely trustworthy, there would be nothing unobtainable to you. This is the reason he keeps you in this unbelieving cycle. Decide that enough is enough. Know that if you can trust God with your eternal destiny, you can trust Him to take care of you and fulfill His plans for you.

Fear

For God has not given us a spirit of fear, but of power and of love and of a sound mind.
II Timothy 1:7 (NKJV)

Fear is a spirit, and it did not come from God. God has not given you the spirit of fear but of faith in Him and His ability. The devil uses fear to keep many of you out of your Promised Land. He used it on the Israelites when they saw giants in the Promised Land that God gave them. Fear kept them from entering. Today his plan of attack has not changed. He is still using fear to intimidate many of you. God has not given you the spirit of fear, but of power, love, and a sound mind. God has given you His power to overcome and annihilate fear. The love that you have for God and others will flush fear out of your life. Many of you have a fear of failure. You must look at the fear of failure in a different light. A failure is not failure, but only an opportunity to learn. When you and I fail at a project, it is a great opportunity to learn what could have been done differently. This failure brings you closer to success because you can put that failed attempt, the thing that did not work, behind you.

For you to stop fearing failure, you must know when you fail you are not a failure. You should not take it personally. You simply failed in your attempt at what you were trying to do, but you are not a failure. You are only a failure when you refuse to try again and to step out in faith. Some of you have a fear of success. You do not believe that you are properly trained to handle the measure of success that will come to you; therefore, you sabotage your own success by not giving your best effort and by not following through on what you originally purposed to do.

Whatever God has pre-wired you to do will bring you to great success. Because He is God and knows all things, He has already determined what is required for you to enjoy your success without it bringing damage to your life. He has already taken you through some challenging situations, which have developed your character so that you will be trustworthy and faithful as He gives you success. God will always put a plan in place so that your success will not cause you to bring shame on His Kingdom. If you trust Him, He will watch over you and govern all the affairs of your life.

One final fear is the fear of what others might think. Sometimes you live life based on the opinions of others. If their opinions are favorable, then you are happy. If not favorable, you can find yourself battling depression. God did not design you to depend on other people's opinions to such a degree that, if they do not agree with you, you are unable to function. Though you can receive wise counsel from others, please keep in mind that the final answer to your destiny must come from God because He is the only One who knows you intimately. Do not let the spirit of fear keep you from reaching higher and attaining all God designed you to attain.

Knowledge/Education

While I was teaching a message recently, I had a revelation that not many men and women in the Bible were college-educated!

This revelation came to light because many of you put limitations on your abilities and yourself. You limit yourself by thinking about what you can and cannot accomplish due to your lack of education and knowledge. God does not qualify or disqualify you because of your education level. He is not looking at what earthly men are looking for when they hire or promote you. God looks at your heart to see if you are trustworthy and can be useable to Him. Some of you have used your lack of knowledge and your lack of education as a hindrance to keep you from moving forward. When God called and chose you, He qualified you to fulfill greatness with your life. He has pre-wired you with everything you need to succeed. You are handpicked and qualified for the tasks that have been assigned to you. Though you may feel limited in your abilities, God has not limited you because of those abilities. I heard these words from a song long ago, which simply said, "If You can use anything, Lord, You can use me." The qualification to be useable is to say, "Yes, Lord," and to surrender your will and your plans over to God. In surrendering, you are saying to God, "I trust Your preparation, and I will be open to however You want to use me to bring glory to Your name."

When God called you to this great destiny, He knew He would have to qualify and prepare you to feel worthy enough, so you would embrace what He has in mind for you. Part of this qualification came when you said "Yes" to Him. With the indwelling presence of the Holy Spirit, you are thoroughly equipped to fulfill every good work. *The Holy Spirit is your teacher and will lead and guide you into all truth (Luke 12:12).* The steps to fulfilling your destiny are in the hands of God, and He will equip and guide you every step of the way. Take the limits off yourself and most definitely take the limits off, God. Understand that there are no ceilings in God.

You can accomplish everything for which He has qualified you. If you can truly believe for it, you can have it no matter your education level or the knowledge you possess. All wisdom comes from God, and it is yours for the asking. God never asks you to fulfill your destiny by yourself. You are the vessel, which He has chosen to pour His power and abilities into, and He will guide you every step of the way.

The Bible says, *"Ask and it will be given to you; seek and you will find; knock and the door will be opened to you"* (Matt. 7:7). To anyone who knocks, God will open the windows of heaven and pour out blessings that you will not have room enough to receive. His power is available to you, and you must decide to receive it.

Outside Influences

You can be hindered and stopped by the influences of others. Many times, you will encounter people, including family and friends, who do not believe that you are truly hearing from God because of the greatness of the destiny He is revealing to you. These outside influences can keep you from fulfilling your destiny because of their belief system. If they do not believe that you are hearing from God, they can deposit their doubt into you, and cause you to question whether you are truly hearing God. Many of you will walk away from your destiny because you do not have the support of your family and friends. You believe if they cannot see the greatness of your destiny, no one else will. That is a lie from the enemy. Most of the time, the people that are closest to you are unable to clearly see because of their foreknowledge of you.

You cannot base your entire destiny on what people think or say because you will miss out on great opportunities every time. Give them the respect of hearing them out but do what the older generation says: "Grind your own meal." Make your own decision.

In the final analysis, God is the only one who knows what you have been equipped to accomplish since He did the equipping.

You can trust that He will not lead you astray but will only lead you down the best path for your life. He is the only influence that you must truly consider. Trust the work He has faithfully begun in you and know that He will not stop until it is fully accomplished. Hear the counsel of your family and friends; but decide that you will base your final decision on the wisest counsel of all, the counsel of the Holy Spirit of God.

Discussion and Reflection

Life Application:

1. Understand there will be hindrances to your destiny.
2. Do not allow these hindrances to stop you from going forward.

Challenges:

1. Fight off doubt, unbelief, and fear.
2. Clothe yourself daily with faith.

Discussion Questions:

1. What hindrances have you encountered on your way to your destiny?
2. How have you overcome these hindrances?
3. Does God have the final say about your destiny?
4. Are you more concerned with your family and friends' opinions instead of the opinion of God?
5. How can you break this cycle of doubt, fear, and the influences of others?

17. FIVE STEPS TO YOUR DESTINY

~

AS I REFLECT ON the reasons God would plan such great destinies for us, I cannot help but think of His great love for us. Because He so loved us, He gave us His very best in the form of His Son. God adores the people He created, and because you are His, there is nothing good that He will ever withhold from you. God is your Abba. He is your Father, and for many of you that is enough, but there are others of you who know Him as Daddy, the One who has been there and has been faithful to you every step of the way. You have intimate knowledge of your Daddy, and He has intimate knowledge of you because you have spent time with Him learning to walk in His footsteps. God is ordering your steps to the special life He has planned for you who fear and reverence Him. He will fulfill the desires of all who stand in awe of His goodness. He is a protective Daddy who watches over every step you take, to keep you from stumbling and falling. If you stumble and fall, He is right there to pick you up and set you on the right path again.

As you get in step with God, He will bring the blessings and greatness from His Kingdom into your life. These blessings are designed to bring fulfillment into your life. When you seek God, and not His blessings, He will pour all His substance into you. The very blessings you long for will be a part of the deposit you receive from Him, as He takes up residency in your life. It is, and always has been, the plan of God that His creation worship and adore Him. As you get closer to Him, every step you take will delight Him. As you delight in giving Him the adoration He so richly deserves, not because of what He has done for you, but because of who He is, you esteem Him greatly. He is absolutely deserving of your highest worship and adoration. As you begin this walk to your destiny, you must take some specific steps. Your first step is to develop a deep intimate relationship with God. Your second step will be obedience to His will and plans for your life. Your third step will be to have faith and confidence in everything He tells you to do. Your fourth step will be commitment to His purposes, and your fifth step will be time spent in His waiting room so that He can perfect His ways in you. Each step will get you closer and closer to God.

Intimacy with God

I want to know Christ and the power of His resurrection and the fellowship of sharing in His sufferings, becoming like Him in His death.
Philippians 3:10 (NIV)

To get in step with God you must have an intimate relationship with Him. In this intimate relationship, you accept Him as your Savior and begin a life of service to Him. There are many people who know Jesus as Savior, but not as Lord. When you accepted Jesus, He came into your life, and you now know that when you die you will spend eternity with Him. There are some people, however, who know Him not only as Savior but also as Lord.

These people have made the decision that they want more than to just spend eternity with God; they desire to know Him in a more intimate way. To know Him intimately, they have submitted and surrendered their entire life to Him. He helps them with every decision whether small or great, and they do not make a move without consulting Him. He has clearance to tell them what to do when to do it, and how to do it. They wait for His okay before moving forward. In their surrendering, they have given everything totally over to His control so He can use them as He desires. The hand of God touches every part of their lives. His signature is on everything they do. When you see them, you see a reflection of God because God is the captain of their souls and the master of their ship. This level of intimacy requires a willingness to submit all that you are and ever will be to the care of a loving God.

Someone defined intimacy as "into me see." God sees your heart and blesses you because He is faithful. As you experience the faithfulness of God, you desire to give Him more and more of yourself. This intimacy is available to all of you, as you yield yourself to God. Tell Him, "Not my will but Your will be done." I challenge you to take a step into this deeper level of intimacy.

Obedience

Then Samuel said: Does the Lord take pleasure in burnt offerings and sacrifices as much as in obeying the Lord? Look: to obey is better than sacrifice, to pay attention is better than the fat of rams.
I Samuel 15:22 (CSB)

Everyone has struggled with obedience. Some of you struggled to obey your parents as you were growing up. I am sure that at times you struggled to obey and submit to instructions from your boss. Many of you have struggled with doing what is right and just. It seems that there is a war going on in you; when you decide to obey and do the things that you are called to do. God does not take pleasure in the things you do or the sacrifices you make. What pleases God is your obedience to Him and doing what He has instructed you to do. The steps of obedience will lead you into a fulfilling destiny, while the steps of disobedience will keep you living below your privileges. To get to any level in God you must learn to hear and obey His instructions. As a young adult, I learned a song that went something like this, "Trust and obey, for there is no other way to be happy in Jesus; you must trust and obey."

For you to experience happiness and fulfillment, you must first learn to hear, trust, and obey the voice of God. God has instructions for each step to your destination. You must have keen ears to hear His voice and then obey His instructions. You learn to hear His voice as you spend time in His Presence. You learn to obey Him when you realize He will never lead you astray and that He has the best plan for your life. Through your disobedience, many of you have taken steps away from God and those steps have led you to pain, heartache, and in some cases destruction. To fulfill everything that God has assigned to your life will require submission to what you hear, and a willingness not only to do what He tells you but also to follow where He leads. To obey God is more beneficial than bringing Him sacrifices which profit nothing. Learn to hear and obey the still small voice of the Holy Spirit. Demonstrate obedience in your conversations and in your walk of life. The steps of obedience will lead you out of mediocrity and into greatness.

Faith/Confidence

Now faith is the reality of what is hoped for, the proof of what is not seen. Hebrews 11:1 (CSB)

Our faith pleases God. In fact, it is impossible to please God without having faith and confidence in Him. In your walk toward your destination, you must not only clothe yourself with humility, but you must also clothe yourself with faith. Faith is the armor, which ensures that you annihilate the attacks of the enemy against you. Faith moves and activates God to go to work on your behalf, and it is the substance that will get you to your destiny. Your faith must be solid and secure in what God has spoken to you about your life. Without absolute confidence in His word and ability, you will not enjoy the richness of your destination. Without faith, many of you merely exist from day to day. Faith gives meaning and life to your existence.

To activate your faith and receive your rewards, you must speak what God has already spoken about you. When you begin to speak His Word back to Him, you activate your faith by kicking it into gear, which brings it roaring to life. In your destiny, you must put action to what you believe. Every act of faith requires movement in the direction of the things for which you believe. You have a voice of faith, which activates your faith as it is used to petition God for the fulfillment of your destiny. Without consistency in speaking God's Word about yourself, you will not experience great success. In your diligence to speak His Word, you must put your heart, soul, mind, and strength behind what you say and believe God to do it.

As a faith-filled person, you cannot be slothful, lazy, casual, or laid-back about your destiny. You must be excited and full of determination to attain anything of significance. Do not be like many who are slothful in their calling and are disengaged and disinterested in what the outcome will be. There are some who look busy on the outside while sitting down on the inside, living life in neutral, going nowhere fast. Your lack of fire and passion is an indication that you do not have the faith or confidence to trust God for the manifestation of His promises in your life.

Your faith must believe regardless of what it looks like in the natural. Faith fights to get the desired result and outcome. You have to make a decision about where your faith address will be. Will your faith address be in the pit of discouragement, despair, lack, loneliness, and fear, or will it be in the blessings, provisions, and favor of the Lord? You must decide if your faith address will be where you benefit the most or where you merely exist from day to day. Whichever of the aforementioned locations you choose to dwell in; will determine the result and outcome of your life. This location will either set the tone for peace and success or stress and unfulfillment. This is a choice you make daily. The step of faith and confidence in the right direction will ensure that you accomplish everything God designed you to accomplish. Have faith and confidence in God. Know that He would not have called and chosen you unless He had already made the necessary deposits in you to accomplish all that He has assigned for your life.

Commitment

Therefore, my beloved brethren, be ye steadfast, unmovable, always abounding in the work of the Lord, forasmuch as you know that your labor is not in vain in the Lord.
1 Corinthians 15:58 (KJV)

Commitment is the glue that keeps you steadfast at your faith address. It ensures that you are not moved regardless of what you hear or see. Commitment is your pledge to God and yourself about what you are contracting and promising to do. Commitment in its simplest form is to do what you say. It is to be entrusted with responsibilities and to have a determination to fulfill them. Your level of commitment is determined by your love for God and your love for what He has called you to do. The level of your confidence in what you hear God saying will also determine your ultimate commitment. This commitment in the preparation process will keep you from straying away from the faith and make you fully available for the highest level of service. Commitment keeps you in the character-building process. It dares to ask the questions, "Are you a person of your word?" and "Do you follow through?" Your character is in a perpetual development cycle based on the commitments you keep. Your words will shape your life and define who you are.

People assess your character as you honor your commitment. Each time you make a commitment and keep it, you die to yourself by putting others first. In your commitment to God, you are willing to sacrifice in order to help others. This allows God to stretch you so that you can grow and develop into the person He birthed you to be.

Commitment is filled with power. Each time you make a commitment and follow through, you demonstrate your obedience to the Spirit of God. Power is released when you place yourself in someone else's difficult shoes and commit to giving them aid. Commitment is one of the greatest responsibilities of your life, without it there would be no corporations, churches, or organizations. It takes committed people to run these enterprises. Your commitment transforms your words and promises into reality. It is making time when there is none and coming through time and again. It is following through when you do not feel like it and realizing that your commitment has the power to transform lives.

Commitment speaks loudly of your intentions and is the stuff character is made of. It is a diehard attitude of never giving up. Commitment is the step that will get you to your destiny and keep you there when the going gets tough. Honoring your commitment to God, yourself, and others can be a step into the most fulfilling and complete life that you could ever imagine.

Time in the Waiting Room

*But they that wait upon the Lord shall renew their strength; they shall
mount up with wings as eagles; they shall run, and not be weary; and
they shall walk, and not faint. Isaiah 40:31 (KJV)*

Have you ever spent time in a hospital waiting room? I have
and it can be an unsettling and sometimes traumatic event. For
many, it is a time of worry, a time of praying, and a time of hoping
for a good report. During my Christian walk, I have discovered
that we will spend much time in the waiting rooms of life. In these
waiting rooms, God continues the process of making you into the
image of His Son. Time spent in the waiting room fashions you to
be of service in the Kingdom. The waiting room is a place where
God begins to do deep work in you to prepare you for your destiny.
It is a time of purging and cleansing to make you fit and useable
by the Master. The waiting room causes your fleshly will and
desires to be crucified so that you can embrace His will and
desires. As you struggle and wait, you truly learn dependency on
God. You learn to trust Him fully for everything by understanding
that only He can give you a breakthrough. Whatever is unnecessary in your life will be stripped away in the waiting room. God
uses this time to trim excess fat and baggage from your life. This
time is Throne time alone with God. Time, when God purges,
cleanses, and purifies you for further use in His kingdom.

The waiting room is a place where negative things that have
been planted in your heart are being uprooted and exposed.
When God begins the exposure, it is an opportunity for you to
face it squarely and decide how to deal with it. God uses the
waiting room of your life to develop your character. This character
development will ensure that when God begins to use you, you
will be ready and equipped to live a life that will bring glory and
honor to Him. In addition, this character development will keep

you steadfast as God promotes you. In the waiting room, you are separated for a season of preparation, and you will learn to totally rest in God.

There was a season in my life when I experienced unemployment and time spent in the waiting room. Since the age of seventeen, I have worked in management, and after college, I took a job in management in Houston, Texas. One year into the job, the economy began to change and my checks from the company started bouncing. After trying to work it out with them, without success, I resigned and was plunged into unemployment. I started my job search and was unsuccessful for a period of time. During this season of unemployment, and time in the waiting room, I discovered several things about myself that God needed to be worked on. When I no longer had a big office to go to, and any employees reporting to me, I was lost. I discovered that I had lost myself in my vocation. When the job ended, I stumbled around like a ship without a sail. I realized that though I had declared for many years that God was my source when the paychecks were no longer coming in, the worry began to set in. I realized that it was very easy to declare that God was my source when checks were coming in, but was He really? If He truly were my source, whether the checks came in or not, He would still supply my needs.

In the waiting room, I discovered that I did not fully trust Him to provide for me. I also discovered that my self-worth and self-image had become so entangled in my vocation that God had to untangle me. He taught me that my value was not in what I did, but in who He had created me to be. After a long time in the waiting room learning these lessons, I thought I was finally ready to embrace a new job assignment. Finally, doors began to open, and the interviews started rolling in. I interviewed for many management positions. Many that I was qualified for, others that I was not, and some that I was overqualified for. Guess what? I did not get even one of those positions. I ended up as an administrative assistant. This was the only door that opened, and I knew that God wanted me to take it.

Now, instead of being in charge, I was the one making the coffee, transferring phone calls, making copies, ordering supplies, and the list goes on. I will be the first to tell you that my ego took a beating, and my attitude needed many adjustments. I was not joyful at all, and even though I was now working, God continued processing me in the waiting room. This time He was working on my humility and my thankfulness in all situations.

Next, He went after my inflated pride. He stripped and stripped until I felt raw and naked, exposed not only to Him but also to myself. When He finished the stripping process, I finally said, "Yes, Lord, what would you have me do to become more like you?" He kept me in that administrative position for almost two years, and each day was a painful time of growth and development. During that period, I began to learn that wherever God sends you, He has an assignment there for you to fulfill. When I stopped looking at my situation in the negative, I began to see the needs of my co-workers and was able to model Christ before them as well as share His faithfulness with them. I was stripped of my pride and ego and began to learn to serve others. Though I felt like the least in this position, I later realized that He was preparing and equipping me with a servant's heart, so that I would humbly serve others. It was a tearful time but a necessary season in my life. Today, He continues to perfect this work in me.

The time in the waiting room with God is absolutely necessary to attain your highest calling. You must trust His timing, His season for you, and His preparation process. In the waiting room of life, learn to yield quickly so that you can learn the lessons, which will prepare and equip you for living life at its fullest.

Discussion and Reflection

Life Application:

1. You must be prepared to take all the steps to your destiny.
2. Time in the waiting room of life is necessary for your equipping.

Challenge:

1. Begin to move in the direction in which God is leading you.
2. Do not fear the process.

Discussion Questions:

1. What steps are you taking toward your destiny?
2. What difficulties are you experiencing along the way?
3. Have you ever been in the waiting room of life before?
4. What did you learn in your waiting room season?
5. How has the experience made you a better person?

18: LIVING IN THE REWARDS AND BLESSINGS OF YOUR DESTINY

~

IT WILL TAKE FAITH to get to your destiny just as it did for Abraham and Joseph. They walked into the fullness of their destinies and enjoyed what God had for them because they operated in faith. When God finally led them to their destinations, it was beyond anything they could ever imagine or dream. They were blessed with abundance in their family life, in their spiritual walk, and their finances. They were spiritually wealthy because they learned total dependence on God. God made their names great throughout the land. They had prominence, they were influential leaders, and they are still highly regarded even today.

Joseph never experienced that degree of loss or lack in his life again. Abraham, through his son Isaac, had children as numerous as the sand on the seashore and the stars in the sky, just as God promised. Abraham became the father of nations and of our faith. Even, his son, Ishmael, who was not the promised heir, prospered and became extremely wealthy just because he was Abraham's seed. Although the journey to their destinies was paved with difficulties, hardships, lack, and loneliness, they did not stop moving forward. They believed they trusted, they waited, and then they walked into a promised land overflowing with all the goodness of God.

Our Rewards and Blessings

It is the greatest plan of God to walk you fully into the rewards and blessings He has reserved for you. He promised in His Word that He would not withhold any good thing from those who walk uprightly before Him (Psalm 84:11b). He is faithful to all His promises, and not one will fail to manifest in your life if you believe Him. To receive your rewards and blessings, you must become like Abraham and Joseph and continue your walk of faith until you get to your faith destination. This destination will be filled with all that you need to be completely satisfied and fulfilled. God is always with you and will be with you throughout the entire journey. He is ready and available to give you all that you have strived and believed for.

The Reward of Peace

Don't worry about anything, but in everything, through prayer and petition with thanksgiving, let your requests be made known to God. And the peace of God, which surpasses every thought, will guard your hearts and your minds in Christ Jesus.
Philippians 4:6–7 (CSB)

Without peace, you will not be able to enjoy the rewards and blessings you receive from God. It takes the peace of God to keep your mind stable and your heart open to receive. A lack of His peace produces anxiety and fear in your heart and mind. These things rob you of the enjoyment of your blessings. When your heart and mind are crowded with cares, it keeps you from finding true rest and hope in a loving and caring God. He desires to give you the Kingdom, and in doing so, He wants you to enjoy all the benefits that come with Kingdom living. In His Kingdom, He fills your heart with His perfect peace, and you find rest for your soul under the shelter of His protection. As you find peace, you live in divine health and prosper in whatever you put your hands to. To ensure you receive and enjoy your rewards, God has provided for your physical health and wealth. Your health starts first with the peace that guards your heart and mind through Christ Jesus. If your mind is healthy and whole, your body will follow suit. When His peace indwells you, you will take care of the body He gave you because you desire to please Him.

God plans to get you to your destiny, and He wants you healthy enough to enjoy every moment of it. It would be unproductive and unfruitful to have gone through all the trials and hardships, and then get to your destiny only to behold it from a distance. How many people do you know who have all the material wealth they could use but are without their health? They are unable to have complete fulfillment because their health keeps them bound and unproductive. When you make peace the umbrella over your life, it will ensure that your health springs forth speedily. The reward of peace will be one of your greatest blessings.

Spiritual Wealth

Beloved, I pray that you may prosper in all things and be in health, just as your soul prospers.
3 John 1:2 (NKJV)

Spiritual wealth is the level of intimacy you have with the Lord, which also brings about soul prosperity. When you spend time cultivating a relationship with Him, He enriches your life with His many provisions. Spiritual wealth is unlimited to those who desire to have it. The more you pursue God, the more He will fill you to overflowing with a wealth of wisdom, knowledge, and grace. Each day, as you walk into His Presence, will be a day you are bestowed with new mercies. You will never truly spend time with God and come away dry or empty-handed. It is impossible. God welcomes you with open arms and lots of joy when you seek after Him. The spiritual wealth you receive as part of your reward and blessing will flood your life with hope, courage, and faith to reach out and grab hold of the goodness of your God. As God rewards you by filling you with Himself, you will begin to look like Him, walk like Him, and talk like Him. When people see you, they will see a reflection of His glory and majesty. This reflection will draw them to you so you can direct them to the Light.

As you continue to develop this spiritual level of intimacy with God, He governs your emotions to ensure that you are whole and complete in Him. Your spiritual development will bring the fulfillment of God to your emotions and relationships. When you obtain this fulfillment, it will bring peace to your life with your spouse, family, children, friends, boss, and co-workers. Spiritual wealth can satisfy every longing in your soul because it comes to you through the person of the Lord Jesus Christ. I encourage you, above all else desire an intimate and abiding relationship with the Lord. This special intimacy will come as you daily schedule time with Him. When you seek Him, you will find Him ready and available to meet your every need and the secret longings of your soul.

Financial Wealth

A good man leaveth an inheritance to his children's children: and the
wealth of the sinner is laid up for the just.
Proverbs 13:22 (KJV)

If they obey and serve Him, they will spend the rest of their days in
prosperity and their years in contentment.
Job 36:11 (NIV)

The above scriptures and many others throughout the Bible make it abundantly clear that God wants you to have wealth and financial blessings. For you to leave an inheritance to your grandchildren, you must have a financial portfolio. God fully intends for you to be blessed financially, to be a blessing to your family, and to have enough left over to give to those in need. He tells you that the wealth of sinners is laid up and set aside for you who are just. When you obey and serve Him, your days will be filled with rest, prosperity, and contentment and He will bring you to your wealthy place. He gives seed to the sower so you can sow into the lives of people who are experiencing financial difficulties. He said, "He who is kind to the poor lends to the Lord, and He will reward him for what he has done" (Proverbs 19:17). You must have something to give to the poor so that they might be sustained. If you do not understand that God desires to bless you with financial wealth, then you are missing out on one of the great promises of the Bible.

When you plant seeds into the lives of others, you experience the fullness of the rewards and blessings that have been reserved with your name on them. These rewards and blessings are reserved for you, so you will have what you need to give as God crosses your path with those whom He wants you to bless. When you spend time seeking the Blesser instead of the blessings, you will have abundance. You receive abundance as you learn to give applause and adoration to God.

As your Father, God desires you to come to Him with praises and thanksgiving on your lips. This attitude of your heart demonstrates to Him that you are fully aware that without Him you could accomplish and attain nothing. This thankfulness ensures that He showers you with more and more blessings. Each time you say, "Thank you, Lord," you acknowledge that you are not equipped to obtain and retain any blessing and reward on your own merit. When you enter the presence of God giving Him the adoration and worship He so richly deserves, you will find an open audience with Him. As God is open and available to you, His rewards come with Him, and He lavishly disperses them.

It is God's ultimate joy to shower His children with blessings. He wants to fill your life with rare and beautiful treasures—treasures in your life, home, job, and your business. He said He will give you every place where you set your foot and that the place will extend from territory to territory and from the river to the great sea (Joshua. 1:3–4). When you receive these precious gifts, you are then able to handle the material and financial abundance He supplies to your life. If you can dream for it, believe for it, and praise Him for it, then you will receive all that your heavenly Father desires to pour into your life. It is my prayer that He opens the reservoirs of heaven and pours you out blessings that you do not have room enough to contain. Pursue Him and you will find all that you need in His presence.

Discussion and Reflection

Life Applications:

1. God has many rewards reserved for you.
2. You must be willing to persevere to get to your destination.

Challenge:

1. Do not stop short of fulfilling your destiny.
2. Embrace every challenge because God is in it with you.

Discussion Questions:

1. How will you know when you have arrived at your destination?
2. What are you willing to do to walk in the rewards and blessings reserved for you?
3. How will you retain your peace and enjoy your destiny?
4. What will you do with the abundant blessings of God?
5. How can you help others achieve their rewards and blessings?

TAKE THE LIMITS OFF YOUR DREAMS

~

"You will not always know what the outcome might be, but you must trust that God will be with you every step of the way. Faith, courage, and hope are key ingredients to your dream-fulfillment. There will be giants along the way that will challenge your faith, hope, and courage, but you have power....."

Joan E. Murray, Author

19: DARE TO DREAM BIG

~

GOD WANTS YOU TO DREAM and to dream big! While God was forming you in the womb, He made deposits of His dream for your life into your heart. This dream is His plan for your destiny. The dream is the purpose for which you were born. God poured visions and dreams into your heart, so you could live a life filled with purpose. Dreams are a picture of the life you can have. They are fantasies of what you can become.

Many of you have sat for hours watching movies you enjoy. These movies bring to life what is in someone's imagination. They take the vision from their imagination and bring it to life with crystal clarity. God has given you a great imagination so you can create pictures or movies of the great life He has planned for you. Your imagination helps you to dream about the future and what you hope to accomplish. The visions you see in your imagination are the outpouring of God's Spirit, which will catapult you into your divine destiny. God has given you the ability to dream as your starting point. Dreams fill your life with purpose and give you a reason to be excited about the opportunities that are ahead of you.

In order for you to dream big, you must step outside of your limited circumstances and embrace something that is far beyond your abilities. You must take the limits off yourself and free your mind to explore the amazing possibilities that can only be found in God. Having a dream will help you face the mountains in your life. Instead of focusing on the mountains, you now dream of the possibilities of what you can both have and become. Every mountain you face must be faced with determination and tenacity if you desire not to be held back from accomplishing your dreams. When you dare to dream big, you will begin to think outside the norm, outside the box. You will be expecting the unexpected around every corner. You will be on the lookout every moment of every day for the manifestation of your dream. You must reach into another dimension and grab hold of every opportunity God has to offer you.

As I began to conduct research about people who have fulfilled great dreams, I found that many of them understood that their dreams were not of their own making but were given to them by God. They acknowledged that a loving God wanted them to prosper and succeed, so He planted great dreams in their hearts. They fully embraced His dreams for them and did everything necessary to fulfill them.

Discovering Your Dream

All of you have been given a dream by God. If you are alive, then you have been given a dream to fulfill. I have often heard it said that the richest place on earth is the graveyard because many people died without accomplishing the dreams that God placed in their hearts. God not only gave you dreams, but He has planned a time frame for their fulfillment. If you are thinking right now, *I don't have a dream,* think again. God did not forget a single one of you as He planted and distributed dreams. You were handpicked and selected to fulfill something in His Kingdom, whether small or great. Something has been stirring in your soul that will not let go of you. Try as you may to bury it, it keeps rising to the surface. This desire to do something is the desire to complete the dream assignment that God so carefully planted in your heart. Many of you have tried to suppress this desire, and you often think you were successful, only to realize later it was only buried for a season. There are others who have used excuses because they believe you are not talented or gifted enough to succeed. You have a hard time believing the things God is speaking to your heart. God is not looking at your talents or gifts because He plans to do the accomplishing through you. If you surrender to Him and to the dream He reveals to you, the dream will indeed come to pass without delay.

You must know God is not going to give you a dream that you can fulfill in your own strength. He never leaves Himself out of the equation of your life. He created you for Himself; therefore, He will always be involved with you in the fulfillment of your dream. To accomplish your God-given dream, you must stop limiting yourself and stop thinking you are not qualified for the task. God has qualified you by the shed blood of His Son. The only approval you need is the stamp of His approval to accomplish what He has deposited in you. It is your right and privilege to dream and to accomplish big dreams. Fulfilling your dream will shine a light on God and bring glory to His name.

The Price to Dream Big

There is a price tag for dreaming big. As you begin to dream, you are often unaware that you will pay a price to accomplish your dreams. I have discovered that many people spend countless hours in the preparation process. Some sacrifice and work tire-lessly to accomplish their dreams; still others must lay down their lives for what they believe. There is always a sacrifice for dreaming big and accomplishing those dreams. The price may look steep as you begin, but the rewards are worth the sacrifice.

The key to success in the dreaming process is to plant seeds into another person's dream while yours is developing. Sow your time into others and help them to overcome the struggles they face while working on their dreams. When you plant seeds into another person's dream and vision, you will reap a harvest in your life when you need it the most. As you begin walking toward your dream, there will be a time of planting, seed time, and harvest. God plants the idea into your heart, you allow the idea to take root and germinate, and then you begin to seed into the idea by plan-ning and preparing to accomplish it. After the planting, there will eventually come a harvest if you do not neglect the seed. You must continue to water it, even during the dry seasons when it appears lifeless.

Beneath the surface of your dreams, growth, and life are taking place even though you cannot see them with the naked eye. There are roots that are growing deep into the soil of your dreams to build a solid and secure foundation upon which you can make something lasting. When the foundation is complete, God will allow you to see the fruit for which you prayed, hoped, and believed. You cannot afford to get impatient and not wait for the full manifestation of your dream. Do not let the enemy rob you of its fulfillment. Remember, God did not miss a single one of you when He handed out dreams. All you have to do is decide to embrace yours and dare to fulfill it.

Discussion and Reflection

Life Application:

1. Dreams are given to you to be accomplished.
2. Believe that your dream is a gift from God.

Challenge:

1. Don't let anyone talk you out of your dreams.
2. Give birth to your dreams by trusting God.

Discussion Questions:

1. What dream has God deposited in your heart?
2. Do you believe that you are called to accomplish it?
3. Are you willing to pay the price to attain your dream?
4. How can you use your imagination to create a picture of your future?
5. What limits you in the fulfillment of your dreams?

20: OBSTACLES TO YOUR DREAMS

~

YOU WILL FACE SOME challenges and obstacles from time to time on your way to the fulfillment of your dream. When you face these challenges, you must make the decision to persevere. Perseverance will be the key that unlocks the door and gives you entry. As you approach your dreams, you may be challenged by lack. Often you may lack the resources you need to begin the process. You may also find that you do not have the necessary help in the beginning phase. Some of you will discover that you may not have the necessary skills or knowledge about where to start. Others' dreams may seem hopeless at first, especially when there are adverse circumstances surrounding them.

You will face some time alone and some loneliness in the process of preparing the groundwork for your dreams. Sometimes when you get to your dreams, it may appear that they are occupied, as was the case with the children of Israel. When they arrived at their Promised Land, giants, unholy, and ungodly people were occupying it; and they knew that it would require a sacrifice and a fight to take occupancy. They had to prepare for outright war in order to take the land. Many of them were faint-hearted not remembering that God was on their side and that He would bring ultimate victory. God is on your side and will bring you ultimate victory, so do not let fear hinder your progress. When you arrive, ask yourself these questions:

- What do I see with my natural as well as my spiritual eyes?
- Do I have what it takes to accomplish it?
- Do I realize that in God it is attainable?
- Do I know the power that I have on my side?
- Can I make a difference in the situations I find?

Every dream will come with problems that you must solve. The problems you encounter will allow you to make a difference by providing aid to those who are without the necessities for survival in our society. You will see many needs, and they will be the reasons for the dream. Each dream that you fulfill will provide a blessing to someone's life. When you see the needs, you must pour all of yourself into their fulfillment. You must pour your passion, heart, and time into making a difference in the lives of those who are around you. Apply your current knowledge or obtain new knowledge to equip you with the right tools for the job. Commit to the hard work that is required for the fulfillment of the dream. You cannot afford to murmur and complain because this will disqualify you.

When the children of Israel came to their Promised Land and saw the giants, they were fearful and believed they could not overcome them, so they began to murmur and complain against God. Their murmuring and complaining led to the death of those who were twenty years and older. Do not let that become your testimony. Murmuring and complaining will break your focus and steal your joy on the journey.

All your dreams will entail a great deal of effort, sacrifice, and planning for their fulfillment. So do everything you can and then trust God with what you cannot. He will provide the help and resources you need. You must begin to enjoy the journey and not be in a race to get to the destination. The journey is a part of the enjoyment of the dream. If you reach your destination and realize that you did not enjoy the process of getting there, you will have missed what God had in store for you along the way. Regardless of what you find when you get to your destination, whether good or bad, do not turn away, face it head-on and decide to accomplish it anyway. God is not surprised by what you will find when you arrive. Therefore, He has already made provision and has planned a victorious outcome for you.

One day I came home from work and was on my way upstairs. As my foot touched the second stair, the Holy Spirit said to me, "You have wasted this day." I stopped on the stairs and began to rehearse all I had accomplished that day. He asked me these questions: "Did you have any joy today?" "Were you smiling and helpful?" "Did you find any pleasure in what you were doing?" I had to answer with a "No" to all His questions. In all honesty, I had dragged through the day without joy, feeling despondent and worrying about things I had no control over. I had allowed those things to steal my joy. The Holy Spirit went on to tell me, "Every day that you are not joyful, peaceful, and content is a day that you have wasted, and you cannot get it back." Enjoy each day it is a gift to you.

Each day is filled with hidden blessings for those who will reach out and grab hold of them. There may be some obstacles to your dreams, but they are worth exploring and overcoming.

Distractions

For we are his workmanship, created in Christ Jesus unto good works,
which God hath before ordained that we should walk in them.
Ephesians 2:10 (KJV)

It is amazing to me that the very moment you decide to get serious about your destiny is the moment when difficulties begin to manifest in your life. You will run into obstacles and situations with your family and friends that call for your immediate attention. The enemy uses distractions to keep you disorientated and unfocused. Distractions break your focus and keep you off-centered. You are then unable to settle in and begin working on the things that are necessary to bring about your destiny. Distractions are a ploy of the enemy to keep you unproductive and in the same cycle day in and day out. You must learn to recognize his tactics and be prepared to counterattack them when necessary. The key to not being caught off guard is to be prayed up and prepared so that as he attempts to distract and dissuade you, you are one step ahead of his ploy. Learn to stay focused when distractions come your way by keeping your eyes fixed on Jesus and continuing to follow the instructions He has given to you. If you focus on Him, you will be able to see the solutions you are looking for quickly and clearly.

Delays

And let us not be weary in well doing: for in due season we shall reap, if
we faint not.
Galatians 6:9 (KJV)

The weapon of delay can bring discouragement to all of us. It appears as if you are always waiting on something. Often you are waiting on God's timing or waiting on help from family and friends or even for the right doors to open for you. In this waiting process, you often feel as if these delays will hamper your progress; but delays are not always denials, and you must learn to stand firm in the waiting season. When you encounter delays, you tend to be less motivated about exploring other options because you are wondering whether it is worth it. Delays keep you believing it was not meant to be, and that nothing good ever happens to you, so why spend the energy trying? The ploy of delays is to keep you living a mediocre existence and to be content with only a limited supply. Delays will keep you from believing that all things are possible with God. You must shake off this weight by pressing into God more and more. Spend time thanking Him for your blessings, which are on the way. Praise Him when you do not yet see the answers. If He has not said "No," then rest assured the answer is definitely on the way. You will get the break-through you need as you learn that perseverance is necessary to get from God what He has in store for you.

Disappointment

Plans fail when there is no counsel, but with many advisers they succeed. Proverbs 15:22 (CSB)

Disappointments come to us in many forms. You might be disappointed because your life is not the way you planned it. Nothing seems to go your way. You keep trying and trying without success, and you just want to yell at the top of your lungs, "Let me off this spinning wheel, this is not what I signed up for." When you are disappointed, you feel sorry for yourself and have some of the greatest pity parties. Poor me, no one cares, nothing I do works! In the midst of your "poor me" syndrome, you cannot feel the encouragement of the Holy Spirit telling you to shake it off and encouraging you to look for the good in all situations. Disappointments cloud your view, and you cannot get a clear picture of where you are or where you are going.

The key to letting go of disappointments is to believe that your steps are ordered by the Lord and that He is leading you to the fulfillment of your dreams. I traveled a lot in a previous job, and many times prior to take off it would be stormy and cloudy on the ground. The moment we rose above the clouds, to our surprise, many times the sun would be shining. God has used this illustration in my life to remind me that the situation is never hopeless, but that I must get a Kingdom perspective on it. My perspective was too limited; therefore, I was limited by it. You are created to press through disappointments and overcome anything that would keep you down and rob the joy of the Lord from your heart. Determine today not to allow disappointments to get the best of you.

Discouragement

Why art thou cast down, O my soul? and why art thou disquieted in me? hope thou in God: for I shall yet praise him for the help of his countenance.
Psalm 42:5 (KJV)

Discouragement comes when fail in your attempts to accomplish something that is of value to you. The enemy tells you that you are the only one who keeps failing and never passing the test. You have to keep in mind that he is a liar and the father of lies. Therefore, do not believe him when he tells you that you are the only one who has missed it. He wants you down and out for the count. When you accept discouragement, you become very lethargic, unconcerned, and unmoved about what is taking place around you. Your courage fails you in the midst of your crisis. Nothing seems to move you, and you are unwilling to give it another try. You give up more easily on your dreams when you are discouraged because you believe you cannot accomplish them. It seems that every time you try nothing happens. You must resist the spirit of discouragement and remind yourself that you are the head and not the tail and that you will not allow it to ruin the plans God has for you.

The Bible tells us that the Kingdom of Heaven suffers violence and the violent take it by force (Matt.11:12). What you need to do is to become violent about the destruction and pain the enemy brings to your life. You must let him know in no uncertain terms that enough is enough, and you will not allow him to continue to rule or control you in any area of your life. You have the power to overcome all things. Tap into your power source and begin to do warfare for the things that have been assigned to you and your loved ones.

Despair

And they overcame him by the blood of the Lamb, and by the word of their testimony; and they loved not their lives unto the death.
Revelation 12:11 (KJV)

Despair is a reality for many people. You suffer despair when you have endured great losses. Despair comes in many forms; and, when you encounter it, you are often unaware of what is going on around you, so you merely exist in a fog. Often you are so lost in despair that you are unconcerned about life and what it still has to offer you. Despair brings a feeling of hopelessness, which can feel unbreakable at times. The enemy's ploy is to keep you so devastated that you cannot run the race that has been set before you. Despair does not have to be a stronghold in your life because you have the power of God on your side to overcome it and keep it from taking up residence in your life. Each day you must decide to fight the spirit of despair and to pull it down. Remember to take every thought captive and bring it under the authority of the Lord Jesus Christ. Take captive the thoughts of despair by submitting them to God who will bring healing and wholeness back to your life.

All these obstacles have been sent to derail you and to keep you from fulfilling your destiny. These things are dream killers, and if you allow them to take root in your heart, they will choke the life out of your dream. The Bible declares that the Greater One lives in you. You have the power to overcome because of the Blood of the Lamb and the word of your testimony (Rev. 12:11). The blood of Jesus purchased your victory at Calvary. Everything that you would ever suffer or endure was nailed to the cross. When Jesus declared, "It is finished," He was telling you everything that would keep you down, discouraged, and keep you from running your race to its completion was annihilated on the cross. All you need to do is believe and accept the gift that has been provided for your success.

You will overcome when you open your mouth and begin to speak the words that He has spoken over you. You are an overcomer because He has made you overcome through His victory at Calvary. You can do all things through Christ who strengthens you. The key to your victory is to begin to act like the son or daughter of the King with all the rights and privileges that come with the position. When the enemy gets wind of the fact that you know who you are; and that you know your rights, He will stop coming around your door and begin to look for others who do not know who they are in Christ. You are a child of the King, and you can make a demand on His Kingdom because He loves you and has reserved the best in life for you.

Discussion and Reflection

Life Application:

1. Know your rights and privileges as a child of the King.
2. Embrace the greatness of the destiny that is yours.

Challenge:

1. Do not allow circumstances to keep you living below your privileges in life.
2. Shake off the obstacles you may face.

Discussion Questions:

1. What obstacles have you faced in your life?
2. What has been the hardest obstacle for you to overcome?
3. What are some things you can do to overcome the five obstacles?
4. Do you know your rights and privileges as a child of the King?
5. How has Jesus provided victory for you?

21: A LIFE-CHANGING DECISION

~

YOU HAVE ALL BEEN given the opportunity to make a life-changing decision at one time or another. This decision has altered the course of your destiny. When God called you to dream big and filled your heart with visions of what you could become, you had the opportunity at that moment to make a life-changing decision. For every dream God has given you, realize that the dream was given to fulfill a purpose in Him. You have been given dreams to meet the needs of others, to bring hope to the hopeless; and to feed the hungry. Your dream will provide shelter for the homeless and clothing for the naked.

God has called you to dream big, so you can be His hands and feet to a world that is in need of Him. As you begin to embrace your dreams and look for the possibilities in them, you must have a willingness to put your all on the line to accomplish them. You will not always know what the outcome might be, but you must trust that God will be with you every step of the way. Faith, courage, and hope are key ingredients to your dream-fulfillment.

There will be giants along the way that will challenge your faith, hope, and courage, but you have the power to look them in the eye and still make the decision that you can do all things through Christ who strengthens you. Do not allow limitations in your dreams or in your thoughts. Be willing to bend and sway with the changes that may come your way. Sometimes changes come to allow you to see a different set of opportunities. You will discover that if you are willing to dream and believe God in the process, then nothing will be impossible for you. The following story will illustrate my point beautifully.

Rahab

Joshua, son of Nun, secretly sent two men as spies from Acacia Grove, saying, "Go and scout the land, especially Jericho." So they left, and they came to the house of a woman, a prostitute named Rahab, and stayed there. The King of Jericho was told, "Look, some of the Israelite men have come here tonight to investigate the land." Then the King of Jericho sent word to Rahab and said, "Bring out the men who came to you and entered your house, for they came to investigate the entire land." But the woman had taken the two men and hidden them. So she said, "Yes, the men did come to me, but I didn't know where they were from. At nightfall, when the gate was about to close, the men went out, and I don't know where they were going. Chase after them quickly, and you can catch up with them!" But she had taken them up to the roof and hidden them among the stalks of flax that she had arranged on the roof.
Joshua 2:1–6 (CSB)

Rahab, a prostitute, made a decision that was to change the course of her life and her destiny. I have concluded she was one of the wisest women in the Bible. She saw an opportunity and grabbed hold of it with both hands. As seen in the above passage, she hid the two spies and kept them from being captured and killed. Once the danger passed, she helped them to escape from one of the windows in her house, using a scarlet rope. Here is why I think she was smart. Before she released them, she extracted a promise from them that when they came in to destroy and take over the city, they would save her and her family. They promised her that if all of her family members were in the house with her, when they came through, and the scarlet cord was hanging from the same window through which she had let them down, her household would be saved.

The scarlet cord is significant in this story because the color of scarlet is bright red. When the Israelites were finally released from captivity, the blood of lambs was applied to the doorposts of their homes. When the Lord swept through Egypt to destroy the first-born sons of the Egyptians, anywhere the blood was applied, the destroyer passed over that house and their first-born sons were saved. When the spies told Rahab to hang the scarlet rope out of the same window, it was to be a reminder to them that, when they approached that house, salvation was to be given to all the occupants in the house. The Israelites came through Jericho and destroyed the city, but Rahab and her family were saved.

Now, get a hold of this picture. The prostitute, Rahab, and her family were taken into the Israeli camp to live among the people. Can you imagine how the prostitute was dressed and what she looked like among those holy, virgin women? God in His infinite grace, mercy, and love had compassion on this prostitute who was willing to be used by Him. Even though she had lived in prostitution, when she encountered God, she allowed God to use the brokenness of her life to bring deliverance to His people. God took her into the Israeli camp, and Salmon, one of the spies who were sent to Jericho, bypassed all the other women in his tribe and married Rahab. One of Joshua's top leaders married the prostitute because it was in God's divine plan. If that was all God did for Rahab that alone would have been a blessing in her life. God, however, did not stop there in His destiny for her.

Rahab and Salmon had children and in Matthew 1, we find Rahab in the genealogy of Jesus Christ. God did not conclude Rahab's story there. In Hebrews 11, you see that Rahab was the only other woman besides Sarah, Abraham's wife, who was listed in the famous Hall of Faith. God took a prostitute who probably had no dream or vision for her life and used the broken pieces not only to deliver His people but to deliver her as well. He forgave, cleansed, and put her on a new path to a destiny she never imagined or dared to dream. He did not waste a single thing that happened in her life. He took all the brokenness, used it for His glory, and then gave her a testimony, which has been told for centuries, just because she was willing to yield to Him. He worked all things together for her good and transformed her life.

As you ponder on the awesomeness of God, consider that if God could use a prostitute to fulfill such greatness to bring glory to Himself, and He is no respecter of persons, then He will do the same for you. All you are required to do is to make a life-changing decision and say "Yes" to Him. He will also take the broken pieces of your life, give you a new dream and vision, and then use you to fulfill the greatest destiny He planned for you before the foundations of the world. He will use you without fail if you will dare to dream big. Like Abraham, Joseph, Rahab, and many other well-known men and women of our time, if you will embrace God's promises, stand on His Word, and never give up, you will accomplish all that you were called, chosen, and destined to do.

Discussion and Reflection

Life Application:

1. You need God.
2. You cannot accomplish your destiny without God.

Challenge:

1. Allow God to use the brokenness of your life for His glory.
2. Don't allow fear to keep you from making a life-changing decision.

Discussion Questions:

1. Have you made a decision to give God your all?
2. How do you know that God can use the brokenness of your life for His glory?
3. What is holding you back from jump-starting your destiny?
4. Have you confessed and released the sins of your past?
5. Have you received the free gift of Christ's salvation?

PRAYER FOR SALVATION

~

FATHER, I know that without You I am lost and without hope. I ask Jesus to come into my life and make His home in me. I repent of my sins and turn back to You. Please forgive me and wash me clean. I open my heart to You and ask You to come and live Your life in and through me. From this day forward, I will live entirely for You. I will not look back on my past but will fully accept Your forgiveness and embrace my future. Thank You that Jesus is now the Savior of my life. Amen!

A PROCLAMATION

~

I AM a child of the King. I will begin to embrace the great plans and destiny He has for my life. I will let nothing stop me from attaining all that He birthed me to accomplish. I will stop living below His promises for my life. From this day forward, I am on a new course to my destiny. I will not be stopped or deterred, and I will live my life to the fullest by honoring God in everything that I do. I will begin my treasure hunt to find out what God has deposited in my life. When I discover His plan for me, I will begin to move toward those plans. I will glorify God in all that I do and bring honor to His Kingdom. Amen!

"YOU CAN TRUST HIM"

ANCHORING YOUR HOPE IN GOD DURING DIFFICULT TIMES

Have you ever faced what seemed like an impossible task? As you looked at what you needed to accomplish, you felt like giving up even before you started. There are seasons in life when we face things that wear us down. These things are designed to stop us from persevering to our victorious end. At times, we have exerted all our strength and are worn out by the effort to accomplish these tasks. In the midst of the struggles, we can get discouraged and may want to quit. Sometimes we feel there is no point in continuing, and if we do decide to continue, we may choose only to put forth the minimum effort. At other times, we may pray for God's help to overcome these obstacles, so we can get better results. During these times you will find God is available to help you. You will also discover what may be impossible for you is definitely possible with Him.

When God gives you an assignment, He fully understands you will need Him in order to successfully accomplish it. He wants to be intricately involved with you in its fulfillment. Ask yourself, "Am I fulfilling my part or attempting to do His part?" Remember, there are things only God can do, and the things He assigns to you, you are capable of handling with His help. Hebrews 10:35-38 says, *"So do not throw away your confidence; it will be richly rewarded. You need to persevere so that when you have done the will of God, you will receive what he has promised."* As you are persevering, you must hold on to your confidence in God. Your journey is not in vain, there is a reward at the end for a job well done. You will receive His promises for your life. Why does God require us to persevere? Because it is developing attitudes in our lives—character, faithfulness, strength, and tenacity. These will help us reach a victorious end and cause us to receive all the promises that are assigned to our lives.

Perseverance helps us get stronger: stronger in our thoughts, emotions, character, and in our physical makeup. Through perseverance, we grow and become better than we were. When God gives us an assignment, He equips us to complete it. If He allows a situation that is causing you to have to press harder towards its accomplishment, then He knows this will produce good fruit in your life. The enemy cannot bring anything into your life that God does not know about. If God allows it to come to you, He knows the fruit this will birth in and through you to impact others for Him.

You Can TRUST Him

NOTES:

1. Chapter 4, 12, 17; Rick Renner, Sparkling Gems from the Greek;
(Tulsa, OK: Teach all Nations, 2003)

2. Chapter 19; The Dream Giver, Bruce Wilkinson
Multnomah Publishers Sisters, Oregon

ABOUT THE AUTHOR

Joan Murray is committed to helping people discover their destinies. She is the founder and CEO of Joan Murray Ministries and Seeds of Hope Worldwide Missions. Joan is dedicated to teaching, training, equipping, and helping people with various life struggles.

Joan is a minister, Bible teacher, author, and missionary. She has traveled extensively throughout the United States and internationally sharing the gospel message and serving the needs of the oppressed. Joan currently resides in Houston, Texas.

If you would like to know more about Joan Murray Ministries or Seeds of Hope Worldwide Missions, please get in touch with us at:

Joan Murray Ministries & Seeds Of Hope Worldwide Missions
26340 FM 1736
Waller, TX 77848
281-398-2501
email: jmmcontactus@gmail.com
website: www.jemmuniquegift.com
website: www.joanmurrayministries.org

Changing Lives Through the Power and Truth of God's Word.

www.ingramcontent.com/pod-product-compliance
Lightning Source LLC
Chambersburg PA
CBHW071320120626
46546CB00002B/383